Quality Rating *and* Improvement System *for* Early Care *and* Education

This book is part of the Peter Lang Education list.
Every volume is peer reviewed and meets
the highest quality standards for content and production.

PETER LANG
New York • Washington, D.C./Baltimore • Bern
Frankfurt • Berlin • Brussels • Vienna • Oxford

Jianping Shen *and* Xin Ma

Quality Rating *and* Improvement System *for* Early Care *and* Education

Development, Implementation, Evaluation and Learning

With Karen Brandi, Jeanne Brossell, Xingyuan Gao, Jeff Goodman, Huilan Y. Krenn, Amy Kavanaugh, Xuejin Lu, Wendy Tackett, Lance Till, Grace Watson *and* Jiangang Xia

In collaboration with the following organizations:
Children's Services Council of Palm Beach County,
Early Learning Coalition, Inc. of Palm Beach County,
Family Central, Inc., Palm Beach State College Institute of Excellence
and the School District of Palm Beach County

PETER LANG
New York • Washington, D.C./Baltimore • Bern
Frankfurt • Berlin • Brussels • Vienna • Oxford

Library of Congress Cataloging-in-Publication Data

Shen, Jianping.
Quality rating and improvement system for early care and education:
development, implementation, evaluation and learning / Jianping Shen, Xin Ma.
pages cm
Includes bibliographical references and index.
1. Early childhood education—United States—Evaluation.
2. Early childhood education—Standards—United States.
3. Child care services—United States—Evaluation.
4. Child care services—Standards—United States. I. Title.
LB1139.25.S54 372.21—dc23 2013011880
ISBN 978-1-4331-2086-2 (hardcover)
ISBN 978-1-4331-2085-5 (paperback)
ISBN 978-1-4539-1120-4 (e-book)

Bibliographic information published by **Die Deutsche Nationalbibliothek**
Die Deutsche Nationalbibliothek lists this publication in the "Deutsche
Nationalbibliografie"; detailed bibliographic data is available
on the Internet at http://dnb.d-nb.de/.

29 Broadway, 18th floor, New York, NY 10006
www.peterlang.com

Table of Contents

Section III. Evaluation of the Quality Rating and Improvement System in Palm Beach County

Section IV. Summary

Acknowledgments

We want to thank the publishers and organizations for the permission to use the materials in the following sources:

Ma, X., Shen, J., Lu, X., Brandi, K., Goodman, J., & Watson, G. (2013). Can quality improvement system improve childcare site performance in school readiness? *Journal of Educational Research* (http://www.tandfonline.com/doi/pdf/10.1080/00220671.2012.667015). Reprinted by permission of Taylor & Francis (http://www.tandfonline.com)

Ma, X., Shen, J., Kavanaugh, A., Lu, X., Brandi, K., Goodman, J., Till, L., & Watson, G. (2011). Effects of quality improvement system on child care centers. *Journal of Research in Childhood Education, 25* (4), 399–414. Reprinted by permission of the Association for Childhood Education International, 1101 16th St., N.W., Ste. 300, Washington, D.C. 20036. Copyright (c) 2012 by the Association.

Shen, J., Ma, X., Tackett, W., Lu, X., Brandi, K., Goodman, J., Till, L., Watson, G. (2011). Effects of quality improvement system on early childhood education practitioners. *Research and Practice Advances in Early Education and Day Care, 15*, 129–154. Copyright (c) by Emerald Group Publishing Limited. Reprinted with permission.

Section I. A National Scene of Quality Rating and Improvement Systems

Section I. A National Scene of Quality Rating and Improvement Systems

1 Quality Rating and Improvement Systems: An Overview

AMY KAVANAUGH

School report cards and rankings have existed for some time as the No Child Left Behind Act of 2002 brought annual testing in mathematics and reading beginning at third grade. Schools and now teachers are evaluated based on student performance on state level standardized tests, and parents pay attention as *US News World Report* releases lists of the top high schools and universities annually. States and the federal government currently emphasize college and career readiness as an overarching goal using teacher quality, student performance, and early childhood education as the foundation for preparing students to succeed (US Department of Education, 2010). Early childhood programs are being touted as a way to prepare students for success related to elementary school academic standards (Brown, 2010; National Forum on Early Childhood Program Evaluation, 2007). It has become clear to parents, educators, and politicians that the continuum of educational experience begins in the first years of life, and high quality child care provides a foundation for the future (Zellman, Perlman, Le, & Setodji, 2008).

Research supports the idea that early care and education can make a difference in students' school performance (Cannon & Karoly, 2007; Child Trends, 2010; Zellman & Perlman, 2008). About twenty-eight percent (28%) of four year olds are enrolled in a state funded preschool (Barnett, Carolan, Fitzgerald & Squires, 2011). Universal preschool is identified as positively affecting numeracy, language and literacy (Weiland & Yoshikawa, 2011). Quality early learning experiences are particularly important for minority groups and children living in poverty as it may increase literacy and social development (Karoly, 2012;Thornburg, Mayfield, Hawks and Fuger, 2009).

It was in the mid-1990s that Dana Friedman discussed skill development for the 21st century and, in turn, the push to increase standards for higher education and high school. The emphasis then included middle school, and elementary levels of education, and finally quality early childhood education. In her opinion it was key that childcare and education reform be linked as children with access to quality childcare are better prepared for academic and social skill development (Friedman, 1994). Early childhood programs impact economics as prevention during childhood is more effective than remediation for adults (Heckman, 2000), and "a growing body of program evaluations shows that early childhood programs have the potential to generate government savings that more than repay their costs and produce returns to society as a whole that outpace most public and private investments" (Kilburn & Karoly, 2008, chap. 3, p. 11). Quality early childhood programs are essentially a strategy to strengthen the economy by saving the government money and leading to societal benefits in the long term (Kilburn & Karoly, 2008).

What Is QRIS?

Quality Rating and Improvement Systems (QRIS) are a set of related reform efforts focusing on continuously assessing and improving childcare and education programs in a local or state context. Various components are used to identify the extent to which a program meets the quality standard. In many cases, part of the assessment result is an easy-to-identify ranking of programs in a local setting or across the state which can be used by parents and funding agencies for decision making purposes. Awareness of QRIS seems to have ramped up in line with the standards movement in education. Comprehensive academic standards exist for kindergarten through twelfth grade in all states as do annual state level assessments in mathematics and reading. Most states (45 states and 3 territories) are now using the common core state standards, and some are voluntarily collaborating on common assessments. In the Reauthorization of the Elementary Secondary Education Act, the Obama Administration calls for the seamless transition of children from early childhood to elementary school programs. In fact, it requires school districts to coordinate with early learning programs and utilize Title I funds to do so.

Table 1.1: *QRIS Components*

*Standards	Process for monitoring	Process for improvement	Financial incentives	Dissemination of information
Supervision: ratios and group size Staff qualifications: staff education levels and professional development	Periodic observations	Technical assistance	Scholarships	Sharing ranking with stakeholders
Learning environment: environmental rating scales and early learning standards	Self reports	Coaching	Grants for continuing education	Marketing
Family involvement	Schedule of assessments Document reviews	Mentoring	Tuition reimbursement Awards	

*The top row is consistent across states, the examples vary by state.

Components of QRIS

Essentially, QRISs have similar elements including "1) quality standards, 2) a process for monitoring standards, 3) a process for supporting quality improvement, 4) provision of financial incentives, and 5) dissemination of information to stakeholders about program quality" (Child Trends, 2010, p. 1).The National Association of Child Care Resource and Referral Agencies also supports these five basic elements (NACCRRA, 2009). Please see Table 1.1 for the QRIS components. The first element, research-based standards, generally governs supervision including group size and teacher/child ratio, staff qualifications, learning environment, and parent involvement. The second element, monitoring quality standards, might include observing, reviewing documents, self reporting, and setting frequency of assessments. The third element is the support for the improvement process, including the provision of technical assistance through coaching and other resources. The fifth element is that financial incentives are used across QRISs to encourage participation but vary by state and include tuition reimbursement, scholarships, and grants for continuing education. Lastly, sharing of information with stakeholders is a consistent element across states. This is mainly used to inform parents about levels of quality across providers (Tout, Zaslow, Halle & Forry, 2009).

There are two main ways in QRISs to identify levels achieved by early childhood programs—building blocks or composite scores (NACCRRA, 2009). Most states involved in QRIS use a building block approach to assign rankings to programs. In 2009, twelve (12) states used this approach. Building blocks means a program meets all the standards for a particular level and must meet all additional expectations to move to a higher level. The building blocks approach allows for stakeholders to more clearly discern how a program performed. A composite score approach is used by fewer states, in which points are assigned to move to the next level of ranking.

Structure and Process

QRIS measures structural and process features of quality. Structural features are those that can be measured quantitatively. Structural features of programs include, for example(a) group size, (b) ratio of students to teacher, (c) caregiver education and training, (d) national accreditation, (e) parental education, and (f) some assessment of the classroom or environment such as Environmental Rating Scales (ERS). Some states include parent involvement and require or incorporate that the center or home has achieved NAEYC or other national accreditation (NACCRRA, 2009; Zellman & Perlman, 2008). The majority of states use the Environmental Rating System (ERS) developed at the University of North Carolina to measure quality of the environment, which includes the Early Childhood Environmental Rating Scale-Revised (ECERS-R) and Infant/Toddler Environmental Rating Scale-Revised (ITERS-R). Only four states do not require the use of an ERS (NACCRRA, 2009). Each of these structural features has had inconsistent outcomes related to quality (Mashburn & Pianta, 2010).Some research supports that size, ratio, and caregiver education and training make a difference in student outcomes (e.g., Volling & Feagans, 1995) while others do not (e.g., Blau,1999).

Process features are qualitative. There features are related to student experience, how the classroom is managed, and students' interactions with caregivers (Kilburn & Karoly, 2008; Zaslow, Anderson, Redd, Wessel, Tarullo, & Burchinal, 2010). Process features often measured include language stimulation and supportive relationship with caregiver/educator (Zaslow et al., 2010). A shift to include more cognitive processes to develop language, literacy, and math concepts has occurred as the research supports the connection to early elementary school readiness (Ladd, Herald & Kochel, 2006; NICHD Early Child Care Research Network, 2002; Trentacosta & Izard, 2007). See Table 1.2 for common domains and how they are assessed. The Caregiver Interaction Scale (CIS) is often used to measure the interactions between student and teacher. This scale includes (a) positive relationship, (b) punitiveness, (c) detachment, and (d) permissiveness (Zellman, Perlman, Le, & Setodji, 2008). The process feature of social interaction in a preschool or childcare setting may be evaluated using the Child Behavior Inventory (CBI), which is a questionnaire administered by classroom teachers to assess children's ability to adapt to and engage in a preschool setting. Teachers rate children on "verbal intelligence, introversion/extroversion, dependence/independence, considerateness, apathy, task orientation, hostility, creativity/curiosity, and distractibility" (Zellman, Perlman, Le, & Setodji, 2008, p. 21). To measure academic stimulation, the Peabody Picture Vocabulary Test is often used to assess receptive language skills. Programs are not required to be nationally accredited but are usually required to be licensed by the state to qualify for the QRIS. Most states have traditional centers and home-based settings that choose to participate in QRIS (Smith, Robbins, Schneider, Kreader & Ong, 2012).

Table 1.2: *Common QRIS Process Features and Assessments*

Domain	Instrument
Student/teacher relationships	Caregiver Interaction Scale (CIS)
Social interaction	Child Behavior Inventory (CBI)
Academic stimulation	Peabody Picture Vocabulary Test (PPVT)

In a study of seventeen statewide QRISs, almost all states reported the use of on-site technical assistance (TA) and coaching to assist with the evaluation process (Smith, Robbins, Schneider, Kreader & Ong, 2012). TA is provided after a center or home participates in the QRIS. Most TA providers used training materials from the Center of Social-Emotional Foundations of Early Learning and the Program for Infant-Toddler Caregivers, common activities included talking about ways to improve and observing caregivers' interactions with children.

The Status of Implementation Across the Nation

History

In the 1950s and 1960s only traditional childcare centers were held to licensing standards, other childcare settings were exempt. During the 1970s centers receiving federal funds were required to follow Program Performance Standards, still in use today (Neugebauer, 2009). The 1980s brought the Early Childhood Program Accreditation project which incorporated NAEYC accreditation as a way to identify quality programs. NAEYC began accrediting early childhood programs in 1985 with its national standards (NAEYC.org). It is a voluntary accreditation program designed to assist parents in making decisions about quality programs for children. It consists of a four-step process: enrollment, application, candidacy, and site visit. An accredited program has a five-year term and then participates in the renewal process. By 1989 the Military Child Care Act was introduced to require quality childcare in Department of Defense childcare centers and homes. The discussion then turned to other measures of quality which led to Quality Rating and Improvement Systems in the late 1990s. The move to standards through the National Education Standards in 2000 and No Child Left Behind in 2002 outlined the knowledge and skills students should demonstrate at particular grade levels. These standards, in turn, emphasized quality early childhood care and education as a way to better prepare children for kindergarten through high school.

In response to the gap between lower level state licensing standards and challenging national accreditation standards, QRIS was developed to highlight quality childcare and learning centers. QRIS began in 1998 when Oklahoma launched an improvement system for childcare centers. The state was seeking to improve the quality of childcare centers by increasing the training of the employees and providing parents with information to evaluate childcare centers. It was comprehensive as it included center compliance with licensing, teacher and director training, weekly lesson plans, use of a daily reading program, staff compensation, parent involvement, and program evaluation. Oklahoma has a universal preschool program which has shown to make a difference in kindergartners' pre-reading and pre-math skills (Karoly, 2012).

Colorado came next, establishing its QRIS in 1999. Colorado's QRIS included staff training and parent involvement, with less emphasis placed on center accreditation but with the addition of child/staff ratios and group size. In 2000 North Carolina began using QRIS, which measured program standards and staff education. Pennsylvania instituted its program in 2002 and Ohio in 2007.

These statewide QRIS include similar inputs, although the emphasis on certain components varies by state. For example, three of the five original states require national accreditation. Each of these early adopter states uses either a star or a step rating system so parents and other stakeholders can identify quality programs at a glance. Parents were not included in the QRIS planning of the early adopter states, but states such as Minnesota have now integrated parent perspective into the quality improvement system (Zellman & Perlman, 2008).

A QRIS Consortium was established in 2006, comprised mainly of early adopter states, to serve as a means to support research and share information across states. As of 2007, 14 states had statewide QRIS in place, and by 2010, the number had climbed to 24 states with statewide QRIS. Nineteen of the states include NAEYC accreditation in some way (NAEYC, 2010). See Table 1.3 for a partial list of states using QRIS as well as summary information related to the scoring systems. States use either a building block or composite score to evaluate programs. The majority of states use building blocks which mean "at each level, a program must meet all requirements of lower levels plus additional specific requirements" (NACCRRA, 2009, p. 7). The composite score is attained by first meeting basic criteria and then points in each category to achieve the next level of quality. Although some states are not listed on Table 3.1, a state may be using a quality improvement system. For example, New York has an evaluation system for the state's Even Start Family Literacy Program, which has consistent structure and process components (New York State Education Department, 2004). Another example, the state of Michigan uses PreSchool Quality Assessment (PQA) through HighScope to evaluate preschool programs according to learning environment, daily routine, teacher-student interaction, curriculum, parent involvement, staff education, and management (HighScope, 2012). Raters use observations and staff interviews to assess program quality and make recommendations for staff development.

At the time of the NACCRRA (2009) publication there were ten additional states described as field testing a QRIS statewide. Research by the National Institute for Early Education Research (NIEER) revealed that Idaho does not currently have a state funded preschool program, and although Arizona has a statewide quality rating system, the state no longer funds the Early Childhood Block Grant to encourage enrollment of children living below the federal poverty level. Mississippi also does not have a state funded preschool program, but Mississippi Building Blocks (MBB), funded by foundations and businesses, has been instrumental in revising quality standards and expectations for preschools since 2008. Nebraska has a state funded preschool program, but it uses "other monitoring" instead of recommended site visits for overseeing quality (Barnett, Carolan, Fitzgerald, & Squires, 2011, p. 91).

Table 1.3: *States or District with QRISs and Scoring Systems*

State or District	Formula	ERS	Accreditation
Colorado	composite	yes	incorporated
Delaware	building blocks	yes	incorporated
Indiana	building blocks	no	required
Iowa	composite	yes	incorporated
Kentucky	building blocks	yes	required
Louisiana	composite	yes	not included
Maine	building blocks	no	required
Maryland	building blocks	yes	required
Montana	building blocks	no	required
New Hampshire	composite	no	required
New Mexico	building blocks	yes	required
North Carolina	composite	yes	not included
Ohio	building blocks	yes	incorporated
Oklahoma	building blocks	yes	required
Pennsylvania	building blocks	yes	incorporated
Rhode Island	building blocks	yes	incorporated
Tennessee	composite	yes	incorporated
Vermont	composite	yes	incorporated
Washington, D.C.	building blocks	yes	required

On the other hand Florida's Voluntary Prekindergarten Education Program (VPK) is available to all four-year-olds where kindergarten readiness assessment data as well as site visits are used to monitor the quality of the program. Minnesota's preschool program meets nine of ten benchmarks from the NIEER's quality standards checklist including benchmarks such as class size, teacher/student ratio, early learning standards, teacher training, and program monitoring. Washington has had state funded preschool through the Early Childhood Education and Assessment Program (ECEAP) since 1985; it also meets nine of ten benchmarks.

The ECEAP, run by the Department of Early Learning, collaborates with the Superintendent of Public Instruction as well as Washington Thrive by Five to provide academics, health, and social services. This program will begin use of a child assessment tool in 2012–2013 (Barnett, Carolan, Fitzgerald, & Squires, 2011).

Kansas has two programs, the Kansas Pre-Kindergarten Pilot Program and At-Risk Four-Year-Old Children Preschool Program; the state is consolidating the two programs into one as well as aligning curricula with early learning standards, reducing teacher/student ratios, and setting expectations for teacher training. Similar to Minnesota, Missouri's Preschool Project (MPP) also meets nine of ten benchmarks set by the National Institute for Early Education Research. The MPP is monitored through site visits, document review, and self-reports, but it was noted the state is developing an evaluation instrument to use across the MPP. Virginia has had a state funded preschool program for at-risk children, Virginia Preschool Initiative (VPI), since 1995. According to Barnett, Carolan, Fitzgerald and Squires (2011), VPI "was evaluated by the University of Virginia and for both process quality and program impact/child outcomes in 2011" (p. 140), and the state department of education does additional monitoring biannually.

According to the National Association of Child Care Resource & Referral Agencies (2009), only five states were not engaged in QRIS at that time—Alabama, Hawaii, Oregon, Texas, and Utah. However, Barnett, Carolan, Fitzgerald and Squires (2011) report that Alabama instituted statewide preschool curriculum standards during the 2011–2012 academic year, and Hawaii has secured US Department of Education's Race to the Top funds to begin funding statewide preschools with the State Advisory Council on Early Care and Education administering the early learning system. Oregon established early learning standards in 2007 and is in the process of revising them; the state uses the federal Head Start requirements as a measurement of quality.The state of Texas began using a quality rating system, School Ready Certification System, in the 2007–2008 school year. It is used in public preschool programs, Head Start, and licensed childcare centers to improve school readiness of preschool students. According to the National Institute for Early Education Research, Utah does not have a state-wide, pre-kindergarten program (Barnett, Carolan, Fitzgerald & Squires, 2011).

There is research that demonstrates QRIS improves the quality of childcare and states have become more interested in whether QRIS impacts children's academic outcomes (Zaslow, Tout, Martinez-Beck, 2010; Zellman & Karoly, 2012). This has occurred as states have begun evaluating the effects of QRIS and parallel to the federal government offering competitive funds through the Race to the Top Early Learning Grants (Mitchell & Cobb, 2011).

Recommendations

The following are the recommendations related to QRIS. First, the initial states to implement QRIS for early childcare and education identified keys to success for the future including securing adequate funding and political support for the QRIS sustainability. Although legislation is not required, agencies that monitor childcare and education can encourage participation, provide marketing, and offer personnel for technical assistance.The technical assistance should be designed to target the quality goals established for the center or home and include progress monitoring related to early math, literacy, language and social-emotional development (Smith, Robbins, Schneider, Kreader & Ong, 2012).

Second, government agencies could play an important role in streamlining the governance structure of QRIS. Raising public awareness of the QRIS has led to parent interest and more childcare and education centers volunteering to be rated. A challenge to address is early childcare and education programs can be fragmented across a state with various agencies holding different responsibilities. Thus, collaboration across agencies is an important consideration for successful implementation of QRIS (Tout, Zaslow, Halle & Forry, 2009; Child Trends, 2010). For example in Michigan,the office of Great Start–Early Childhood is now located at the Department of Education and will coordinate 84 separate early childhood funding sources that were previously managed through different state agencies (Snyder, 2011).

Third, common understanding of what it means to be ready for kindergarten should be established by educators and policymakers as various definitions exist (Brown, 2010). The expected skills and behaviors need to be developmentally appropriate for children and assessed by early childhood instructors and caregivers. Similarly, the diversity of children served including culture, language, and age, as well as type of program, home-based or center-based, need to be considered for measuring quality across different settings.

Fourth, given the various typologies of implementation in various states, it is difficult to compare across the states. However, over time, successful typologies of implementation will emerge. A past president of NAEYC, Anne Mitchell, commented that if states integrated the national standards into QRISs it would streamline the process and encourage comparison of programs across state lines (as quoted in Neugebauer, 2009). Many states use the ten program standards established by NAEYC within their QRISs, but at different capacities. Another challenge is that variations in programs make it difficult to make consistent recommendations across the nation. Even if states use ERS, the weighting and number of classrooms observed are different (Tout, Zaslow, Halle & Forry, 2009). Although it may be confusing to have different QRISs by state, perhaps in time the most successful will rise to the top and serve as models for other states. Multiple means of measuring quality is important, and, therefore, national accreditation and state level QRISs are viable ways to improve, identify, and report quality early childhood programs.

Finally, the NACCRRA (2009) recommends that strong licensing regulations and oversight need to be in place for a successful QRIS, and states need to recognize accreditation from various organizations as well as require the following: " . . . a license for all paid providers who care for unrelated children . . . , background checks for all licensed providers . . . , and unannounced inspections for technical assistance" (p. 11). Stakeholders need to be involved in the development and implementation of a QRIS including parents, educators, administrators, child care resource agencies, and other appropriate human services organizations. This can help ensure that research-based practices are utilized to establish the strongest QRIS.

References

Barnett, W.S., Carolan, M.E., Fitzgerald, J., & Squires, J.H. (2011). *The state of preschool 2011: State preschool yearbook.* New Brunswick, NJ: National Institute for Early Education Research.

Blau, D. M. (1999). Effect of child care characteristics on child development. *The Journal of Human Resources, 34*(4), 786–822.

Brown, C. (2010). Balancing the readiness equation. *Journal of Early Childhood Research, 8* 2, 133–160. doi:10.1177/1476718x09345504.

Cannon, J.S., Karoly, L.A. (2007). Who *is ahead and who is behind? Gaps in student achievement in the early grades for California's children.* Santa Monica, CA: Rand Corporation.

Child Trends. (May 10, 2010). Quality rating and improvement systems for early care and education. *Early Childhood Highlights, 1*(1), 1–4.

Friedman, D. (1994). Business and early childhood education reform. *Theory into Practice, 33*(4), 235–241.

Heckman, J.J. (2000). Policies to foster human capital. *Research in Economics, 54*(1), 3–56.

HighScope. (2012). *Preschool Program Quality Assessment (PQA).* Retrieved from http://www.highscope.org/Content.asp?ContentId=116

International Reading Association-National Institute of Child Health and Human Development. (2005). *Conference on early childhood literacy research: A summary of presentations and discussions.* Retrieved from http://education.ucf.edu/mirc/Research/IRA-NICHD_summary.pdf

Karoly, L.A. (February 2012). *Building blocks for a strong preschool to early elementary education system.* Paper presented before the Council of the District of Columbia, Committee of the Whole.

Kilburn, R., & Karoly, L.A. (2008). *The economics of early childhood policy: What the dismal science has to say about investing in children.* Santa Monica, CA: Rand Corporation.

Ladd, G. W., Herald , S. L. & Kochel , K. P. (2006). School readiness: Are there social prerequisites? *Early Education and Development,* 17, 115–150.

Mashburn, A. J. & Pianta, R. (2010). Opportunity in early education: Improving teacher-child interactions and child outcomes. In A. Reynolds, A. Rolnick, M. Englund, & J. Temple (Eds.), *Childhood programs and practices in the first decade of life: A human capital integration.* New York: Cambridge University Press. pp. 243–265.

Mitchell, A. & Cobb, G. (September, 2011). Quality rating and improvement systems (QRIS) and Head Start alignment: A discussion paper. QRIS National Learning Network. Retrieved from http://qrisnetwork.org/sites/all/files/resources/gscobb/2011–10–06%2006:35/QRIS%20Head%20Start%20Alignment.pdf

NAEYC. (2010). *Public policy fact sheet.* Retrieved from http://www.naeyc.org/files/naeyc/file/policy/state/QRSFactSheet.pdf

National Association of Child Care Resource & Referral Agencies (NACCRRA). (2009). *Comparison of quality rating and improvement systems (QRIS) with Department of Defense standards for quality.* Retrieved from http://www.naccrra.org/sites/default/files/default_site_pages/2011/army_qris_state_report_081709.pdf

National Forum on Early Childhood Program Evaluation. (2007). *Early childhood education program evaluations: A decision-makers guide.* Retrieved from http://www.developingchild.harvard.edu/content/downloads/Decision_Guide.pdf.

Neugebauer, R. (March/April 2009). Where are we headed with center accreditation? Trends in quality assurance. *Child Care Exchange, 178,* 14–17.

NICHD Early Child Care Research Network (2002). Early child care and children's development prior to school entry: Results from the NICHD Study of Early Child Care. *American Educational Research Journal, 39,* 133-164.

New York State Education Department. (2004). *New York State Even Start Family Literacy Performance Indicator Manual.* Retrieved fromwww.p12.nysed.gov/evenstart

Smith, S., Robbins, T., Schneider, W., Kreader, J.L., Ong, C. (2012). *Coaching and quality assistance in quality rating and improvement systems: Approaches used by TA providers to improve quality in early care and education programs and home-based settings.* New York, NY: National Center for Children in Poverty, Mailman School of Public Health, Columbia University.

Snyder, R. (2011, April 27). *A special message from Governor Rick Snyder: Education reform.* Lansing, MI: State of Michigan Executive Office.

Thornburg, K.R., Mayfield, W.A., Hawks, J.S., & Fuger, K.L. (2009). *The Missouri quality rating systems school readiness study: Executive summary.* Kansas City, MO: Center for Family Policy & Research University of Missouri and the Institute for Human Development University of Missouri. Available at: http://cfpr.missouri.edu/MOQRIS.pdf.

Tout, K., Zaslow, M., Halle, T., & Forry, N. (2009, May). *Issues for the next decade of quality rating and improvement systems* (Issue Brief No. 3). Washington, DC: Office of Planning, Research and Evaluation Child Trends.

Trentacosta, C. J., & Izard, C. E. (2007). Kindergarten children's emotional competence as a predictor of their academic competence in first grade. *Emotion, 7,* 77–88.

US Department of Education. (2010). *Reauthorization of ESEA: A blueprint for reform.* Retrieved from: http://www2.ed.gov/policy/elsec/leg/blueprint/index.html

Volling, B.L. & Feagans, L.V. (1995). Infant day care and children's social competence. *Infant Behavior and Development, 18*(2), 177–188.

Weiland, C. & Yoshikawa, H. (2011). *The impact of an urban universal public prekindergarten program on children's early numeracy, language, literacy, and executive function outcomes.* Paper presented at the 2011 SREE Conference, Washington, DC.

Zaslow, M., Anderson, R., Redd, Z., Wessel, J., Tarullo, L., & Burchinal, M. (2010). *Quality dosage, thresholds and features in early childhood settings: A review of the literature, OPRE 2011–5.* Washington, DC: Office of Planning, Research and Evaluation, Administration for Children and Families, US Department of Health and Human Services.

Zaslow, M., Tout, K., & Martinez-Beck, I. (2010). *Measuring the quality of early care and education programs at the intersection of research, policy, and practice,* OPRE Research-to-Policy, Research-to-Practice Brief OPRE 2011–10a. Washington, DC: Office of Planning, Research and Evaluation, Administration for Children and Families, U.S. Department of Health and Human Services.

Zellman, G.L. & Karoly, L.A. (2012). *Moving to Outcomes: Approaches to incorporating child assessments into state early childhood quality rating andimprovement initiatives. Santa Monica, CA: RAND Corporation.*

Zellman, G.L. & Perlman, M. (2008). *Child care quality rating and improvement systems in five pioneer states: Implementation issues and lessons learned.* Santa Monica, CA: RAND Corporation.

Zellman, G.L., Perlman, M., Le, V.N., & Setodji, C.M. (2008). *Assessing the validity of the qualistar early learning quality rating and improvement system as a tool for improving child-care quality.* Santa Monica, CA: RAND Corporation.

2

Issues in Designing, Implementing, and Evaluating Quality Rating and Improvement Systems

AMY KAVANAUGH

The landmark 40-year study of at-risk children who participated in high quality preschool in Michigan revealed that they had higher rates of employment and earnings, lower rates of crimes committed, and were more likely to have graduated from high school than children who did not have access to preschool (Schweinhart, Montie, Xiang, Barnett, Belfield, & Nores, 2005). Parents, school leaders, economists, and policy makers generally agree that high quality preschool is important to the future. Over the last decade, all but two states have adopted early learning standards for programs. In 2001–2002 only one third of the states had these standards; in 2011 the last two states were in the process of developing standards.Still, state funding has declined in 26 of 39 states with preschool programs (Barnett, Carolan, Fitzgerald & Squires, 2011).

Quality rating and improvement systems (QRIS) for early care and education programs began with a state-sponsored system in Oklahoma in 1998, a privately sponsored system in Colorado the following year, nineteen statewide QRIS by 2009, and almost half of the states in the process of developing QRIS (NACCRRA, 2009). What began as a rating system for parents now emphasizes both *ratings* and *improvement* processes for early childhood programs. The Alliance for Early Childhood Finance touted QRIS as the first step toward statewide accountability and governance of early childhood care and education programs (Mitchell, 2005); at that time there were ten states using QRIS. One can see the parallel growth of accountability in K-12 education with annual assessments associated with NCLB. The Obama administration's Race to the Top Early Learning Challenge through the Reauthorization of the Elementary and Secondary Education Act emphasizes quality and provides opportunities to replace the loss in state funding for preschool programming, including QRIS.

Issues in Designing and Implementing QRIS

There are a number of states that instigated quality rating and improvement systems earlier than most. Colorado, North Carolina, Oklahoma, Ohio, and Pennsylvania are referred to as the pioneer states and have identified learnings related to implementation that can be drawn on by other states in the process of QRIS (Zellman & Perlman, 2008). Reflecting on their ground-breaking work with QRIS, these states have implementation recommendations related to field testing, components to include in the quality rating systems, quality improvement processes, and the communication of quality rating levels attained. Based on the literature, the following is a summary of issues and learnings related to designing and implementing QRIS.

Getting Started

Interestingly, setting standards can prove complicated for QRIS. The idea is to set high standards of quality for programs to reach. However, states found that exceedingly high standards discouraged participation beyond the basic licensing level. States in the planning process of QRIS need to carefully field test the program. This means making any necessary changes before the program goes live to rate and improve early childcare and education programs. States with QRIS reported that it was important to avoid making changes to the QRIS program after implementation. Changes after the fact led to confusion and frustration on the part of the participants across the states. Naturally, these feelings hinder buy-in on the part of the childcare and education programs. States that field tested and prepared participants for minimal changes reported more success. It is wise to take time up front to try the program before going state-wide.

Components in QRIS

Pioneer states also had similar, specific recommendations related to components to include in QRIS. State licensing should be included in any QRIS. For example, if a provider is licensed, its program should meet the minimum requirements for QRIS. By beginning with licensed programs QRIS can focus on indicators of quality beyond basic safety. It was also recommended that national accreditation not be mandatory. States reported that the high cost of national accreditation prevented some viable programs from seeking the accreditation and possibly qualifying for QRIS (Zellman & Perlman, 2008). In addition to the high cost, national accreditation also took more time to attain and delayed rating because another organization was involved in reviewing the program.

In a QRIS there are generally self-reported data as well as data collected by independent assessors who visit programs for information gathering. The states agreed that limiting the self-reported data is a key to getting a clear picture of a program. Although expensive due to the training of raters, Environmental Rating Scales (ERS) and other similar instruments should specifically be used as independent assessments at different levels within the QRIS. This is especially true in high-stakes situations where funding and other incentives are tied to quality, because self-reporting may involve bias. This conclusion parallels the careful reporting of k-12 student test data during the time of NCLB. States have specific guidelines for collecting, using, and distributing state-level assessment data.

Another component to include in the implementation of a QRIS is multiple levels across the continuum of expectations for quality. A program at the peak of the QRIS should still strive to demonstrate growth and progress instead of mere maintenance of quality. Technical assistance should be available across the quality levels for programs to improve in target areas. Research supports the use of professional development paired with coaching to improve language and literacy instruction in early childhood programs (Sandefur, Warren, Gamble, Holcombe, & Hicks, 2010).

Quality Improvement Processes

The improvement system is an important part of the QRIS and mainly includes staff development and financial incentives to support growth. The financial incentives include reimbursement for children who receive state subsidy, scholarships for staff continuing education, professional development programs, and staff retention incentives. Programs that demonstrate quality earn financial incentives to perpetuate quality. Resources need to be available to improve the quality of all programs, especially those that service the most at-risk children.

States suggest the use of separate raters and quality improvement personnel. Rating and coaching should be done by different people to avoid conflict of interest or bias. Most states recommend annual monitoring of programs, not necessarily rating annually, as this frequency allowed for quality improvement to take place. Technical assistance (TA) should be offered at the pre-application phase and after a rating. The pre-application TA includes, among other things, "classroom observations and assessments in order to advise staff about how to improve quality; providing guidance about how to obtain grants to support quality assistance; training staff on classroom quality assessment tools" and developing a plan to prepare for the assessment process (Smith, Robbins, Schneider, Kreader, & Ong, 2012, p. 7). After a QRIS rating is given, TA should emphasize what needs to be done to move up in quality levels. Most frequently TA providers focused on "efforts to improve the classroom or environment. . .practices that promote social-emotional growth, language development, and early literacy growth" (Smith, Robbins, Schneider, Kreader, & Ong, 2012, p. 8). TA is commonly provided by talking with teachers and directors and observing teachers in action. Other effective strategies for TA are guidance with planning and modeling of instruction so teachers can see effective strategies in action. TA providers found that it was difficult to visit programs more than once per month. Assistance with coaching should ideally occur frequently for teachers and directors to effect changes within the programs and improve quality.

Communication of Quality Rating Levels

The rating levels are public knowledge and should be shared with parents, so they can make informed decisions regarding childcare and education. Zellman and Perlman (2008) reported that ongoing marketing is important to introduce and define the quality rating system, detail the components, and identify the quality level attained. The marketing should begin after the QRIS is field tested to avoid confusion if changes are made to the system. Ideally, parents should not have to research the information which could be marketed to them through media, health care providers, and religious and socialization activities. Childcare and education programs are usually proud of their ratings and share that information with prospective parents. They also share that the QRIS is but one evaluation of the program, a practice that may also hinder parental understanding of QRIS.

Alignment

A core issue related to the implementation of a QRIS is the preparation of young children for pre-school and early elementary school. NCLB led to state level academic standards and early learning standards which now exist in the form of the

Common Core State Standards adopted by 45 states. It is important that the pre-school learning standards align with the elementary school standards so the transition from pre-school to kindergarten is seamless. Karoly (2012) advocates the alignment of standards, curricula, assessments, and professional development for teachers. The emphasis on learning outcomes from kindergarten through secondary school begins in pre-school or even earlier. In addition to alignment of pre-school through elementary learning standards is the alignment of QRIS assessment measures with program goals as well as weighting, and validation (Zaslow, Tout, & Martinez-Beck, 2010).

The goals of QRIS currently vary by state and, more recently, include whether children are progressing toward kindergarten readiness, whereas the earlier emphasis was on process or structural measures of quality. Tools for measurement of academic development may now include the Classroom Assessment Scoring System (CLASS) and the Early Literacy and Language Classroom Observation (ELLCO), in addition to the Environment Rating Scales (ERS) used to measure process or structural elements. Once the tools for measurement of program quality are identified, the formula for arriving at a composite score is determined. This composite score could encompass process and structural features as well as possible child development outcomes. The ways to arrive at the composite score also vary by QRIS.

Validating measures is another component of alignment within implementation of QRIS. Consistently measuring quality across different care and educational settings is complex as parents may choose to use a childcare center, licensed home day-care, or care by family or neighbors. Center-based care is held to a different standard as it is more conducive to the instructional and observation requirements. Establishing program goals, aligning measurement tools with the goals, identifying the process for arriving at composite scores, and then validating scores across different settings is all part of implementing a QRIS. Alignment is a far reaching issue in the implementation of QRIS as program goals need to connect with selected measures as well as elementary learning standards. Perhaps a remedy is to draw upon stakeholders across states similar to that of Common Core State Standards. This collaboration would allow for easier comparison of quality across the country.

Issues in Evaluating QRIS

Quality rating and improvement systems are on the rise as many states have implemented them to rate and rank the early care and education programs available for children. There are complexities, however, related to the evaluation of QRIS within and across states including variation in programs, diverse subgroups, integration of child assessment data, and logic models.

Variation

The variety of observational tools, financial incentives, and inclusion of different program types in QRIS makes it difficult to draw conclusions about QRIS across the country (Tout, Zaslow, Halle & Forry, 2009). Within each QRIS observational tools are used to assess the learning environment; many, but not all, states use the Environmental Rating Scales (ERS) which include Early Childhood Environmental Rating Scales as well as Infant/Toddler Environmental Rating Scales. Of the states that employ ERS for home and center QRIS, there are then variations in the number of classrooms observed. Other states may use additional scales including the Classroom Assessment Scoring System (CLASS). The differences in QRISs across the country continue into the financial area as rewards in the form of scholarships, grants, and bonuses are earned for serving low-income children, the quality level achieved, and other stipulations, depending on the system. Lastly, the types of early childcare and education programs included in state QRISs vary by state. Typically, all licensed programs can participate in a state's QRIS, which includes center and home-based programs. Head Start and state-run preschools may or may not be eligible. The ages of children included in such programs may include infants, toddlers, or school-aged children.

Diverse Subgroups

The differences among state-wide QRISs is profound including participation of types of programs (e.g., center or home-based, licensed or state-run) and the children in these programs. States may consider whether the standards for center-based or home-based programs should look different. Participating children vary in age, socioeconomic status, culture, and language. As the United States becomes more culturally and linguistically diverse, so do the children participating in early care and education programs. The planners of QRISs need to be cognizant of the diverse families participating in early care and education programs. Consideration for learning supports to assist the particular needs of children participating is important for their developmental growth. Communication with parents of diverse children needs to be planned as well so they can use the QRIS to be informed. The diversity of various subgroups, including both the programs and children in these programs, poses a challenge to QRIS evaluation.

Child Assessments

High quality early childhood care and education programs have demonstrated increases in pre-reading and pre-math skills for children entering kindergarten (Karoly, 2012). Initially quality rating and improvement systems for early childhood programs were designed to provide information to parents and funders, feedback and technical assistance for program employees, and financial incentives to improve. Research on QRIS is somewhat limited and until recently focused mainly on elements over outcomes of the programs (Tout, Zaslow, Halle & Forry, 2009). The evaluation questions usually targeted which programs enrolled in QRIS, which programs showed improvement over time, and parent use of quality rating resources. Traditionally, states have emphasized measuring the inputs into early childhood programs which may or may not contribute to child functioning. The structural and process features of an early childhood program are unlikely to get at child development or performance issues. Structural features generally encompass classroom learning environment as measured by various versions of ERS, child-staff ratios, staff training, and parent involvement. Process features of early care and education programs refer to, among others, "warmth, sensitivity, and stimulation that characterize child-staff interactions" (Zellman, Perlman, Le, & Setodji, 2008, p. 19).

Given the more current goal of QRIS to improve the quality of care and "identify child cognitive, social, emotional and physical functioning," there are a variety of strategies that are being explored to integrate the assessment of child functioning into the QRIS (RAND, 2012, p. 4). Assessments of child functioning have been deemed too expensive or complicated to connect child outcomes to a particular input or features. However, Colorado, Indiana, Minnesota, and Missouri each seek to measure change in student outcomes (Tout, Zaslow, Halle & Forry, 2009). Unlike K-12 education which assesses student learning with standardized tests, early childhood programs have difficulty identifying assessments to use as young children have limited attention spans and stranger anxiety (Zellman & Karoly, 2012).

Nevertheless, Zellman and Karoly (2012) highlight the importance of integration of assessments as children's development is the true measure of quality. They suggest five particular approaches to including assessments of child development into state quality rating and improvement systems: (a) caregiver/teacher assessments to improve practice, (b) QRIS required caregiver/teacher assessments to improve practice, (c) independent measurement of child outcomes to assess programs, (d) independent measurement of child outcomes to assess QRIS validity, and (e) independent measurement of child outcomes to evaluate programs.

The first approach of "caregiver/teacher assessments to improve practice" can be used to target employee needs for professional development and improvement of care and instruction. The second approach of "QRIS required caregiver/teacher assessments to improve practice" differs from the first one as it would be a requirement for reaching the upper tiers of a QRIS. The third approach to assessment incorporates the use of trained assessors to collect developmental data to identify program effectiveness. This is more difficult as it is expensive and is methodologically complex; this approach has not been implemented by statewide QRIS to date. In the fourth approach, independent measurement of child outcomes to assess QRIS validity, trained assessors collect child developmental data to "determine if programs with higher QRIS ratings produce larger developmental gains for participating children" (RAND, 2012, p. 2).This approach is being used by some states with a sample of children and is, therefore, less expensive than the third approach. The final approach to integrating child assessments, "independent measurement to evaluate programs", is expensive and complex, but has the potential to be used to evaluate the overall impact of early childhood programs at the state level. Zellman and Karoly (2012) recommend independent assessors use child data to identify causal effects of particular programs as compared to state outcomes. However, they caution that this approach be field tested before being used statewide.

Logic Models

Before launching an evaluation of the state QRIS, the U.S. Department of Health and Human Services Office of Planning, Research and Evaluation proposes the development of a logic model to illustrate the potential achievements of a QRIS. Since the proposed quality achievements may vary by state, the logic model provides a pictorial or flowchart of the stakeholders' intentions. For example, one state may set the goal as improving child cognitive outcomes and another may target childcare services. The logic model is a useful tool to clarify the goals of a QRIS and demonstrate how the activities and resources lead to the goals. According to Lugo-Gil, Sattar, Ross, Boller, Tout, and Kirby (2011), "logic models depict the links between the environment, the intervention, and the changes in the environment that result from the intervention" (p. 3). The logic model shows the intended resultant outcomes, among others.

The logic model commonly includes resources, activities and then outcomes that result from the activities. QRIS logic models tend to be more detailed to incorporate external influences that impact resources and activities such as those that are social or political. The outcomes section of a QRIS logic model is divided into outputs, "measureable direct results of activities" and "more distant outcomes for providers, families, and children" such as quality of care and improved child cognitive outcomes (Lugo-Gil, Sattar, Ross, Boller, Tout & Kirby, 2011, p. 5).

QRIS is a meaningful approach to the improvement and evaluation of early childhood care and education programs across the country. States are increasingly using this potentially comprehensive approach to improvement. The issues surrounding design, implementation and evaluation of QRIS as well as learnings from states that were early adopters of QRIS can be used to design even stronger systems in the future.

In the following chapters, the Children's Services Council of Palm Beach County's program is used as an example to illustrate the design, implementation, and evaluation of a QRIS at the county level (chapters 3, 4, 5), evaluate the QRIS with outcomes related to the early care and education practitioners, monitor quality of the early care and education sites (including both homes and centers), and children's school readiness level (chapters 6, 7, 8 and 9), and the major learnings from Children's Services Council of Palm Beach County's efforts (chapter 10). We hope that the successful case illustrated in the book will be constructive for those who embark on a similar endeavor.

References

Barnett, W.S., Carolan, M.E., Fitzgerald, J., Squires, J.H. (2011). *National Institute for Early Education Research: The state of preschool 2011 executive summary.*

Karoly, L.A. (February, 2012). *Building blocks for a strong preschool to early elementary education system.* Paper presented before the Council of the District of Columbia, Committee of the Whole.

Lugo-Gil, J., Sattar, S., Ross, C., Boller, K., Tout, K. & Kirby, G. (2011). The Quality Rating and Improvement System (QRIS) Evaluation Toolkit: OPRE Report #2011–31. Washington, DC: U.S. Department of Health and Human Services, Administration for Children and Families, Office of Planning, Research and Evaluation.

Mitchell, A. W. (2005). A guide for states and communities developing quality rating systems for early care and education.Collins Management Consulting & United Way of America Success by 6.

National Association of Child Care Resource & Referral Agencies (NACCRRA). (2009). *Comparison of quality rating and improvement systems (QRIS) with Department of Defense standards for quality.*

RAND Corporation (2012). *Incorporating Child Assessments into State Early Childhood Quality Improvement Initiatives Research Brief 9639-PF.*Retrieved from http://www.rand.org/content/dam/rand/pubs/research_briefs/2012/RAND_RB9639.pdf

Sandefur, S.J., Warren, A.R., Gamble, A.B., Holcombe, J.M., & Hicks, H.K. (2010). Coaching: It's not just for Little League. In S.B. Neuman & M.L. Kamil (Eds.), *Preparing teachers for the early childhood classroom: Proven models and key principles* (pp. 87–103). Baltimore: Paul H. Brookes Publishing Co.

Schweinhart, L.J., Montie, J., Xiang, Z., Barnett, W.S., Belfield, C.R. & Nores, M. (2005). *Lifetime effects: The High/Scope Perry Preschool study through age 40.* Ypsilanti, MI: High/Scope Press.

Smith, S., Robbins, T., Schneider, W., Kreader, J.L., Ong, C. (2012).*Coaching and quality assistance in quality rating and improvement systems: Approaches used by TA providers to improve quality in early care and education programs and home-based settings.* New York, NY: National Center for Children in Poverty, Mailman School of Public Health, Columbia University.

Tout, K., Zaslow, M., Halle, T., & Forry, N. (2009 May). *Issues for the next decade of quality rating and improvement systems* (Issue Brief No. 3). Washington, DC: Office of Planning, Research and Evaluation Child Trends.

Zaslow, M., Tout, K., & Martinez-Beck, I. (2010). *Measuring the Quality of Early Care and Education Programs at the Intersection of Research, Policy, and Practice, OPRE Research-to-Policy, Research-to-Practice Brief OPRE 2011–10a.* Washington, DC: Office of Planning, Research and Evaluation, Administration for Children and Families, U.S. Department of Health and Human Services.

Zellman, G.L., & Perlman, M. (2008).*Child care quality rating and improvement systems in five pioneer states: Implementation issues and lessons learned.* Santa Monica, CA: RAND Corporation.

Zellman, G.L., & Karoly, L.A. (2012).*Moving to outcomes: Approaches to incorporating child assessments into state early childhood quality rating and improvement systems.* Santa Monica, CA: RAND Corporation, OP-364-PF.

Zellman, G.L., Perlman, M., Le, V.N., Setodji, C.M. (2008). *Assessing the validity of the qualistar early learning quality rating and improvement system as a tool for improving child-care quality.* Santa Monica, CA: RAND Corporation.

Section II. Designing and Implementing the Quality Rating and Improvement System

3

The Quality Improvement System in Palm Beach County: A Brief Introduction

JIANPING SHEN, WENDY TACKETT, XIN MA, XUEJIN LU, KAREN BRANDI, JEANNE BROSSELL

Background Information

Although definitions of high quality sometimes vary across societies as a result of different perceptions of childhood and the purpose of ELCC (early learning and childcare), a general consensus has emerged in the early learning and childcare literature that specific conditions are essential at the system level to ensure that high quality at the program level is the norm rather than the exception. (Friendly, Doherty, & Beach, 2006, p. 15)

Although there currently are no national standards for a quality improvement system, many state childcare agencies have chosen to look systematically at a set of goals that are linked in the research to quality. Some of the key objectives of the state agencies include promoting healthy childcare environments, providing training and formal education for providers and programs, strengthening professional development systems, and increasing emotionally supportive caregiving (Pittard, Zaslow, Lavelle, & Porter, 2006).

The Palm Beach County Quality Improvement System (QIS) is a comprehensive, voluntary, early care and education improvement system that seeks to enhance the quality of childcare so that children from birth to age 5 will be healthy and ready to learn when they enter school. A number of recent studies have proven that high-quality early childhood experiences are a major factor in children's development and ability to succeed once they reach school and even later in life. The research predicts that every dollar spent on quality early childhood education will save $7 later in reduced special education, welfare, and prison costs.

Taking into account this and other research, as well as the large number of working families needing childcare, a group of local early childhood advocates worked for over a year to design a comprehensive, customized early care and education quality improvement system for licensed childcare sites, school-based childcare sites, and family childcare homes who hold a rate agreement with Family Central to accept children receiving subsidies. Collaboration participants included the Children's Services Council of Palm Beach County; Early Learning Coalition of Palm Beach County; Palm Beach Community College; School District of Palm Beach County; Family Central, Inc.; Palm Beach County Health Department; Health Care District of Palm Beach County; Palm Beach County Child Care Directors Association; Palm Beach County Family Child Care Association; and individual childcare sites and family child care providers. The group incorporated lessons learned from a local pilot program, the Picower Quality Child Care Initiative, and national quality initiatives. The QIS of Palm Beach County was finalized in 2003 with the following goals:

1. To produce positive outcomes for children;
2. To provide consumer education to help parents recognize, expect and seek out quality in a childcare setting; and,
3. To define, advocate for, and obtain the resources necessary to encourage, support, and promote quality early care and education.

The Palm Beach County's QIS consists of a number of components, including:

1. Six Pathways to Quality,
2. Achievable Standards,
3. Star Ratings,
4. Reliable Assessments,
5. Quality Improvement Supports, and
6. Consumer Education Opportunities.

These components work together to create a supportive quality improvement system that leads to good outcomes for children. A brief overview of each component is provided below.

1. **Six Pathways to Quality** are proven predictors of quality focusing on:

- Environment
- Professional Development
- Staff-to-Child Ratio and Group Size *(applying to childcare centers and school-based child care sites only)*
- Administration and Business Management *(applying to family childcare homes only)*
- Parent Involvement
- Program (Curriculum)
- Child Developmental Screenings

Each of the Six Pathways to Quality has achievable standards that are assessed and reported using a weighted formula that gives a childcare site its "star rating." The assessment results are used to develop individualized improvement plans. The two key pathways to quality are Environment and Professional Development, and they are each given more weight in the assessment results. The other pathways are called the "Supporting Pathways to Quality," and they are given slightly less weight in determining a childcare site's star rating. All of the pathways contribute to quality in an early care and education setting.

2. **Achievable Standards** are contained in each of the six Pathways; four levels that correlate with the one- to four-star ratings. These standards provide a fair system for assessing and rating a childcare site as well as a roadmap for achieving high quality.

3. **Star Ratings** indicate to what extent a childcare site has met general quality criteria. Star ratings can increase as higher standards are met up to a four-star rating. A one-star rating, in general, means that a childcare site has only met basic licensing standards. An overall star rating is awarded after each formal assessment. Although the star rating is an important aspect of the Quality Improvement System, a childcare site's commitment to continuous improvement is the key to success and upward progress through the Quality Improvement System.

4. **Reliable Assessments** ensure a fair, consistent, and accurate assessment process for each participating childcare site. A nationally recognized, research-based program assessment tool called the Environment Rating Scale is used to assess and rate a childcare site's environment. To assess the other pathways, qualified and highly reliable program assessors use on-site care observations as well as documentation from the provider. A childcare site's first assessment is the baseline assessment; no star is awarded at this point. The results of the baseline assessments are used by

an Early Learning Coach (ELC) and the director/family childcare provider to create an individual quality improvement plan. After a childcare site has been in the QIS for a year, a reassessment is conducted. Results from this second assessment are used to create a quality maintenance plan and determine a star rating. Quality enhancement payments begin after a childcare site has been in the QIS for one year and the second assessment has been completed.

5. **Supports** are available to childcare sites and their staff participating in the Quality Improvement System. These include, but are not limited to, on-site technical assistance provided by highly trained and experienced ELCs; reliable assessments done by program assessors; director and staff professional development opportunities; scholarships; mini grants; peer networking opportunities; quality enhancement payments to childcare sites; educational incentive awards; wage supplements; and individual career advising for directors and staff.

6. **Consumer Education Opportunities** and materials are provided to inform current and future parents and staff of a childcare site's commitment to enhanced quality through its participation in the QIS. These marketing materials help parents recognize, choose, and expect quality in an early care and education setting.

QIS is a complex design. For more details on the design and implementation of QIS, please refer to the next section on QIS theory of change and the logic model.

QIS Theory of Change and Logic Model

Systems Thinking as the Underlying Rationale for QIS

Systems thinking is the underlying rationale for the design of QIS (Kim, 2002; Senge, 2006). First, QIS illustrates that a system is more than the sum of its components—a basic tenet of systems thinking. The interconnectedness of the programs and clusters is the key to producing effects at the system level. Second, the design of QIS is generative rather than reactive. Too often we respond to a complex issue with a simple solution. QIS recognizes the dynamic complexity in improving early care and education and generates a dynamic and complex system to improve early care and education. There is always a gap between the current reality and the ideal situation, and the gap becomes a creative tension that leads to a generative orientation to creating QIS. In the case of QIS, the gap does not lead to a reactive orientation with focus on what to avoid. Rather, CSC staff and QIS partners focus on what to create. Finally, the reinforcing mechanism embedded in the relationship among all QIS partners also embodies the core theory of success of systems thinking (Berkley, 2004).

Figure 3.1: *Quality Improvement System Logic Model*

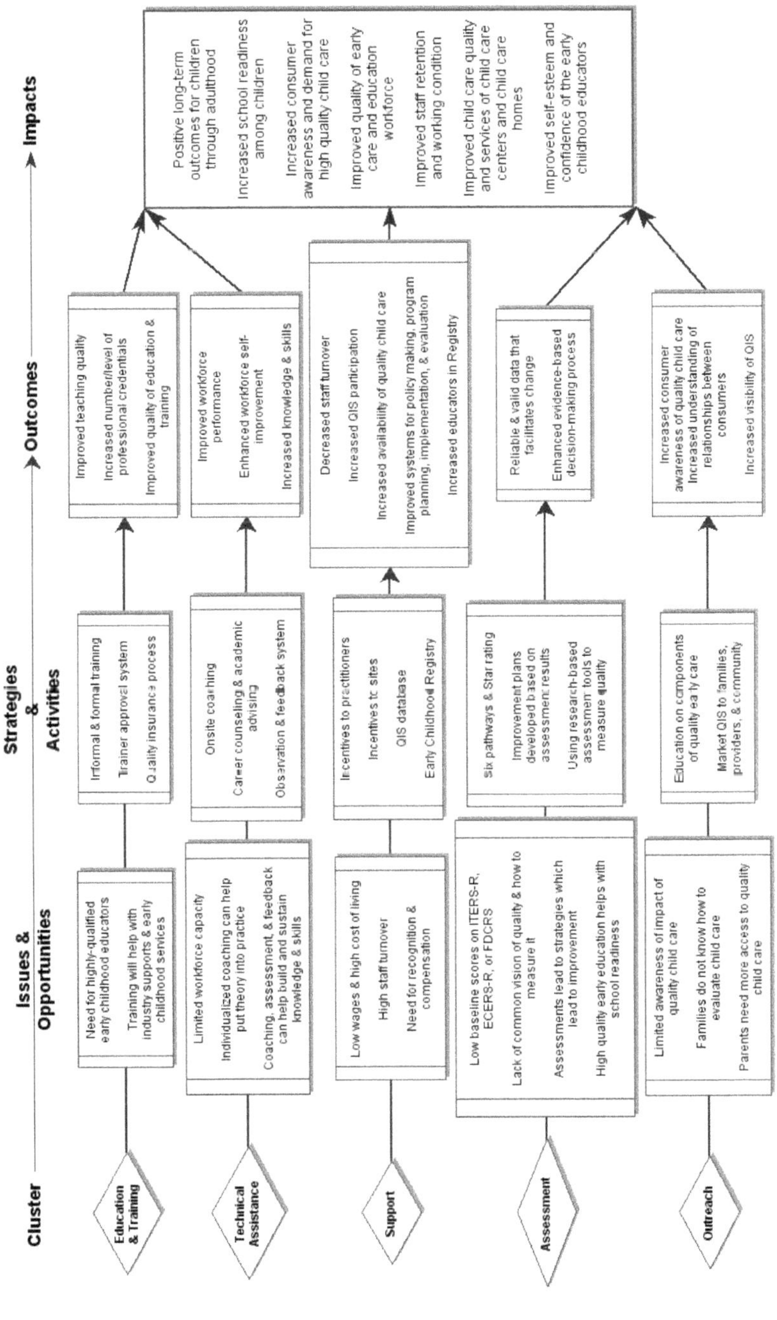

To construct QIS from a systems thinking perspective maximizes the likelihood of the impact at the system level. However, because QIS is itself a complex system that is nested in an even larger and more complex system, it takes time to see the components work together to create the synergistic impact at the system level. Furthermore, when the impacts of QIS take place, it is also difficult, and sometimes virtually impossible, to point out a single source for the impact at the system level.

QIS Logic Model

The QIS logic model has four major components: (a) issues and opportunities, (b) strategies/activities, (c) outcomes, and (d) impacts. In the *issues and opportunities* component, the logic model identifies major issues facing QIS and major opportunities available to address those issues. In the *strategies* component, the model lays out the key strategies and activities that QIS is adopting to tackle the issues facing quality child care. In the *outcomes* and *impacts* components, the model specifies the expected outcomes, respectively, for the QIS. The *outcomes* and *impacts* will provide the tangible and intangible targets for all the QIS evaluators involved. The success of the overall QIS may be evaluated by examining the extent to which the designed outcomes and impacts for the participants at different levels are obtained (see Figure 3.1).

Approaches to Evaluating QIS

Purpose of the QIS Evaluation

The key objectives of the QIS evaluation are (a) *improvement*—to provide data and information to support and facilitate the improvement of the system; (b) *accountability*—to provide evidence on the effectiveness and impact of the system; and (c) *knowledge*—to allow for the acquisition of a more profound understanding in some specific area used to inform policy and manage system changes. This implies understanding both the *outcomes* of the system and the *process of implementation.* Overall, the purpose of the QIS evaluation is to help us learn as much as possible about the entire system, as well as what has worked, what has not worked, and how to improve it.

Description of the QIS Evaluation Model and Plan

In order to support the childcare providers to enhance quality of childcare, the QIS identified the following five key strategies: (a) education and training of child care workforce; (b) on-site technical assistance of ELCs to the rated sites for improving quality based on an assessment of site needs; (c) implementation of the assessment process using a four-star rating system for childcare sites; (d) financial incentives and supports for quality improvement; and (e) outreach for public and consumer awareness of quality childcare. These strategies are expected to (a) improve the preparation, qualifications, and teaching performance of the childcare workforce; (b) enhance the capacity of child care providers and their staff to improve the level of their star ratings and the quality of child care provided; (c) increase the use of reliable assessment data for child care program improvement; (d) improve staff retention and working conditions; and (e) increase public support for child care quality improvement and increase both parents' awareness of child care quality and their motivation to seek out and pay for quality care. The evaluation is designed to examine both the implementation and the effectiveness of these five key QIS strategies and the overall effectiveness of the system.

Figure 3.2: *Palm Beach County Quality Improvement System*

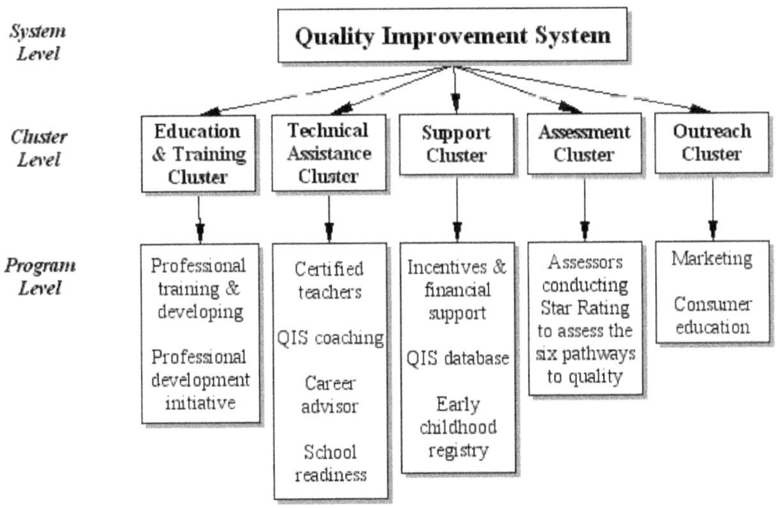

The multilevel nature of the QIS is illustrated in Figure 3.2 (Yang, Shen, Cao, & Warfield, 2004; Shen, Yang, Cao, & Warfield, 2008). At the base level are individual programs or activities, doing the work designed to improve quality childcare. All these programs and activities are grouped into five clusters based on the five identified strategies: education and training, technical assistance, support, assessment, and outreach. The education and training cluster consists of programs and activities that provide and coordinate formal and informal professional development and curriculum training to early childhood workforce in the QIS. The technical assistance cluster contains programs and activities in which ELCs provide intensive, on-site coaching and assistance to childcare providers and teachers to improve the performance of the childcare sites and the level of their star ratings. The support cluster consists of financial incentives (scholarships, quality enhancement payments, wage supplement, awards), the QIS database, and the training registry. The assessment cluster includes the star rating system, which focuses on assessing, communicating, and improving the level of quality of childcare sites based on the standards of the six pathways to quality. The outreach cluster includes activities such as marketing, networking, and outreaching that are meant to increase public and consumers' awareness and access to quality care. Finally, at the top level, the QIS covers all five clusters.

According to this alignment model, evaluation of the QIS will be conducted at the three different levels: the program level, the cluster level and the system level. At the base level, the program evaluation focuses on the performance of the individual program or activity. At the middle level, the cluster evaluation examines the performance of each of the five clusters. At the system level, the evaluation assesses the success or lack of success of the entire system.

The CIPP Model for Process and Product Evaluation

For the evaluation, the external evaluators adopted the CIPP model, with an emphasis on the process and product evaluation. CIPP stands for context, input, process and product. The CIPP Model was developed by Daniel Stufflebeam (1966, 1983) and is a widely used model for program evaluation, among others. The foci of the CIPP model are as follows (Stufflebeam, 2003, 2007):

- *Context* evaluation assesses needs, problems, assets, and opportunities within a defined environment.
- *Input* evaluation assesses competing strategies and the work plans and budgets of the selected approach to assess feasibility and cost-effectiveness.
- *Process* evaluation monitors, documents, and assesses program activities.
- *Product* evaluation identifies and assesses outcomes—intended and unintended, short term and long term—to help program staff focus on achieving outcomes and help the stakeholders gauge the program's success in

meeting target needs. Product evaluation has the following elements: impact, effectiveness, sustainability, and transportability.

Given the fact that QIS has been in place for a few years and that QIS staff and stakeholders have been implementing the theory of change for QIS, the external evaluators chose to focus on the process and product of QIS. Therefore, the external evaluators asked pertinent process and product (outcome) questions for the overall QIS and each cluster.

The Following Chapters

The next two chapters (chapters 4 and 5) give more details on Palm Beach County's QIS as well as general principles of designing and implementing a QIS. Chapters 6, 7, 8, and 9 provide evaluation results on (a) the impact of QIS on practitioners, (b) the effect of QIS on childcare sites' quality, (c) the impact of QIS on site-level children's school readiness, and (d) the overall strengths and weakness as perceived by the practitioners in participating childcare sites. The final chapter (chapter 10) summarizes the major learnings from designing and implementing Palm Beach County's QIS.

References

Berkley, A. (2004, November). *Systems thinking in the foundation world: An example from the W. K. Kellogg Foundation.* Paper presented at the American Evaluation Association, Atlanta, Georgia.

Cohen, J., & Cohen, P. (1983). *Applied multiple regression/correlation analysis in behavioural sciences* (2nd ed.). Hillsdale, NJ: Erlbaum.

Friendly, M., Doherty, G., & Beach, J. (2006). *Quality by design: What do we know about quality in early learning and child care, and what do we think?* Toronto, Ontario, Canada: Child Resource and Research Unit, University of Toronto.

Kim, D. H. (2002). *Organizing for learning: Strategies for knowledge creation and enduring change.* Waltham, MA: Pegasus Communications.

Moreno, R. (2008). *Description and analysis of the Florida Kindergarten Readiness Screener (FLKERS) and the Kindergarten Readiness Rate: Accountability Measures for the Voluntary Prekindergarten Program in the State of Florida.* West Palm Beach, FL: Palm Beach Community College

Pittard, M., Zaslow, M., Lavelle, B., & Porter, T. (2006). *Investing in quality: A survey of state child care and development fund initiatives.* Washington, DC: National Association of State Child Care Administrators and Child Trends with the Bank Street College of Education.

Rosenthal, R., & Rosnow, R. L. (1984). *Essentials of behavioral research: Methods and data analysis.* New York: McGraw-Hill.

Senge, P. M. (2006). *The fifth discipline: The art and practice of the learning organization* (rev. ed.). New York: Doubleday/Currency.

Shen, J., Yang, H., Cao, H., Warfield, C. (2008). The fidelity–adaptation relationship in non-evidence-based programs and its implication for program evaluation. *Evaluation, 14* (4), 467–481.

Stufflebeam, D. L. (1966). A depth study of the evaluation requirement. *Theory into Practice, 5* (3), 121–133.

Stufflebeam, D. L. (1983). The CIPP model for program evaluation. In G. F. Madaus, M. Scriven, & D. L. Stufflebeam (Eds.), *Evaluation models* (pp. 117–141). Boston: Kluwer-Nijhoff.

Sufflebeam, D. L. (2003). *The CIPP model for evaluation.* Paper presented at the Annual Conference of the Oregon Program Evaluators Network (OPEN), Portland, Oregon. Retrieved August 2, 2008, from http://www.wmich.edu/evalctr/pubs/CIPP-Model Oregon10–03.pdf

Stufflebeam, D. L. (2007). *CIPP evaluation model checklist.* Kalamazoo, MI: Evaluation Checklists Project. Retrieved August 2, 2008, from http://www.wmich.edu/evalctr/checklists

Yang, H., Shen, J., Cao, H., & Warfield, C. (2004). Multilevel evaluation alignment: An explication of a four-step model. *American Journal of Evaluation, 25* (4), 493–507.

4

The Design of the Quality Improvement System

XIN MA, JIANPING SHEN, IN COLLABORATION WITH CHILDREN'S SERVICES COUNCIL OF PALM BEACH COUNTY, EARLY LEARNING COALITION, INC. OF PALM BEACH COUNTY, FAMILY CENTRAL, INC., PALM BEACH STATE COLLEGE INSTITUTE OF EXCELLENCE, AND THE SCHOOL DISTRICT OF PALM BEACH COUNTY

Design Principles for Quality Improvement System

With more and more societal emphasis on early childhood education to prepare children for successful schooling, an urgent need clearly emerges to understand and facilitate healthy child development during the period of early childhood. What skills, abilities, knowledge, and behaviors do children need to develop in early childhood education to ensure school success? How can practitioners and care centers create caring and learning environments rich in activities that promote child development in those areas? These questions must be addressed in any design of QIS (Quality Improvement System). In other words, these questions are the starting point for designing any QIS.

A growing national trend for promoting and ensuring the quality of early childhood education is for early caring and learning to join the standards movement (Scott-Little, Kagan, & Frelow, 2003). In a nutshell, the standards movement prescribes clear, standardized expectations for what children must know and must be able to do at the exit of an educational program (e.g., elementary mathematics education). The standards movement has proliferated across the entire formal K-12 education, with curriculum, instruction, and assessment standards developed for almost all school subjects.

The *Head Start Child Development and Early Learning Framework* is the latest federal effort in developing early learning standards (Head Start Resource Center, 2011). Other highly regarded national early learning standards are the *Pre-Kindergarten Standards: Guidelines for Teaching and Learning* (CTB/McGraw-Hill, 2003) and the *Early Childhood Program Standards* (National Association for the Education of Young Children [NAEYC], 2008). Most states are on their way to establish similar standards to measure child learning outcomes as a result of early childhood education (Child Care Bureau, 2006). These national and state efforts aim to develop explicit expectations for child learning outcomes.

Standards come with two different frameworks. Most existing standards are behavior-based, and they prescribe clearly defined cognitive and affective behaviors that children are expected to exhibit upon the completion of a topic, a unit, or a grade in a certain educational program. The Head Start standards fall into this category. Unique about CTB/McGraw-Hill (2003) is that behavior-based standards are converted into effectiveness-driven pedagogies. This category then emphasizes teacher behaviors (in teaching practices) more than child behaviors (in learning outcomes). One way or the other, these frameworks are resources and guidelines that help administrators and practitioners identify elements necessary for providing quality programs for children before they enter kindergarten (formal education).

The importance of standards is highlighted in Figure 4.1 as the centerpiece for system design of any QIS. We refer to Figure 4.1 as our matrix model of system design. There are five components in the model: standards, practitioners, centers, children, and parents. Standards are the foundation, and all other components are built upon and around the centerpiece of standards. In the remainder of this chapter, we provide more detail on each component and supplement our discussion with experiences from the Palm Beach QIS.

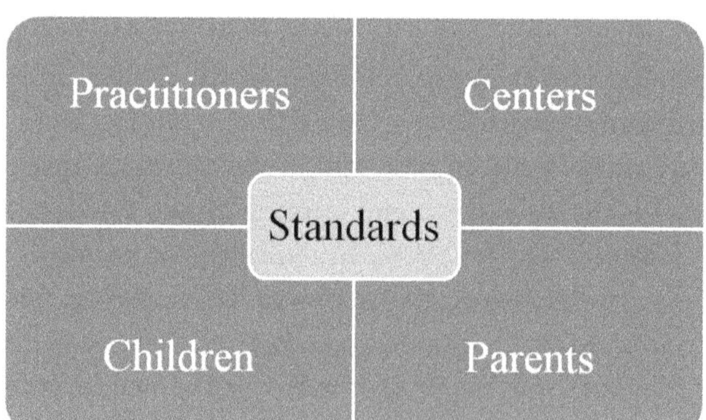

Figure 4.1: Matrix Model of System Design

Standards

We believe that standards for early child education should govern learning environments, learning outcomes, curriculum and instruction, assessments, and professionalism. The national standards that we briefly discussed earlier target comprehensively and systematically learning outcomes, curriculum and instruction, and assessments. Most standards at the state level mirror these national standards. The design of local QIS should consult and adopt these standards as the core to ensure that learning outcomes, curriculum and instruction, and assessments are up to the state (national) standards. What is relatively weak in national and state standards pertains to learning environment and professionalism. We thus provide some discussions on these issues to guide the development of standards for the design of local QIS.

We normally do not find any standards on learning environments in formal education. It should, however, be a critical part of any standards for early childhood education because of the recognition that young children learn most effectively from authentic experiential interactions with their environments (e.g., Virginia Department of Education, 2010). Children in early childhood have more curiosity about their surroundings than those in any other age group. For example, the importance of learning environments to language development is emphasized (Head Start Resource Center, 2011). To some extent, learning environments must be considered part of standards for early childhood education also because of the caring function of childcare facilities that demands a careful establishment of the environments in which children spend a chunk of their daily time.

Learning environments for early childhood education must be achievable yet challenging for all children (NAEYC, 2008). Operationally, we believe that learning environments for early childhood education must be rich cognitively, affectively, and interpersonally. Interpersonal interactions are needed for caring and for learning. Standards for interpersonal interactions are much harder to define because caring and learning needs change so frequently and quickly that a standard prescription for practitioners is almost impossible. Nevertheless, the essence is that practitioners must spend sufficient quality time with each child to care for his or her needs and to personalize activities for the purposes of learning. In other words, we believe that time is the major element in standards for interpersonal interactions. When developing these standards, there is a need to separate time for routine caring and learning from time that is devoted to "teachable moments" referring to the opportunities either purposefully designed or entirely spontaneous that are able to lead children to a much deeper understanding or appreciation of certain knowledge. Routine time is necessary and important, but practitioners should mindfully design or sensitively seize personal teachable moments to engage each child in a much deeper understanding or appreciation of certain achievable yet challenging knowledge.

Cognitively effective learning environments should be well organized, equipped, and maintained. Organization refers to the arrangement of furniture in such a way that allows easy navigation for both practitioners and children. The display of toys and educational materials should stimulate children to explore (e.g., to ask questions). Walls and ceilings are good space to arouse children's curiosity. Equipment refers to the availability of essential teaching and learning means such as an exploring corner (for simple science), a classroom library, a system of audio and video devices, and computers facilitating interactions with educational software packages. Maintenance refers to the regular repair and update of organization and equipment.

Affectively effective learning environments rely on the emotion, attitude, and confidence of practitioners. Practitioners should offer emotional support for children to feel welcomed and valued, and children should be able to feel that practitioners are dependable for their caring and learning needs. Practitioners are important role models to children, and as such they should demonstrate at all times positive attitudes toward learning and great confidence in overcoming difficulties and challenges in caring and particularly learning activities.

Learning environment is one of the Pathways to Quality in the Palm Beach QIS, based on the belief that design and maintenance of the physical environment support high quality program activities and services and allow for optimal use and operation. Their position is that well organized, equipped, and maintained environments support program quality by facilitating the learning, comfort, health, and safety of those who use the program. In addition, a welcoming and accessible setting for children, families, and staff enhances program quality (NAEYC, 2008).

The Palm Beach QIS uses a three-week window to assess learning environment of childcare centers in one day or over several days. The Infant/Toddler Environment Rating Scale–Revised (ITERS-R) is used to assess classrooms in which the majority of children are at age of 0 to 30 months, whereas the Early Childhood Environment Rating Scale–Revised (ECERS-R) is used to assess classrooms in which the majority of children are at age of 30 months and above. Developed by researchers at the University of North Carolina at Chapel Hill, ITERS and ECERS are designed to gauge various quality indicators of group programs for children. Both ITERS and ECERS assess six indicators of learning environments (i.e., there are six subscales on learning environment): space and furnishings, personal care routines, listening and talking (ITERS) or language reasoning (ECERS), activities, interaction, and program structure. One third of the total classrooms are randomly assessed at each center, with at least one ITERS room and one ECERS room randomly chosen for assessment. A program's average ITERS or ECERS score becomes what the Palm Beach QIS refers to as environment pathway score that counts for 40% of the program's final star rating. Appendix 4A presents star ratings for the learning environment as a pathway to quality.

Professional standards are not commonly addressed in formal education, although there are such standards in, say, mathematics education. We introduce the *Professional Standards for Teaching Mathematics* (National Council of Teachers of Mathematics, 1991) as an example that may help establish similar professional standards for early childhood education. We have removed those mathematically specific terms to make the professional standards more general. The essence of the professional standards speaks to the important decisions that teachers need to make in their teaching: selecting and using worthwhile tasks; managing classroom discourse; creating an environment to support teaching and learning; and analyzing student learning, tasks, and environments to make instructional decisions. These professional standards are achieved through professional development of teachers. The standards for professional development emphasize knowledge on content and pedagogy: modeling sound teaching of content, knowing both discipline content (e.g., mathematics as an academic discipline) and school content (e.g., mathematics as a school subject), knowing students as learners of content, developing as teachers of content, and promoting teachers' role in professional development.

Staff qualification and professional development are also pathways to quality in the Palm Beach QIS, arguing that children benefit most from teachers who are knowledgeable in early childhood development and provide developmentally appropriate activities in response to the individual needs of children. As an ongoing process of continuous improvement that increases job related knowledge and skills, the Palm Beach QIS provides structured teaching and learning experiences for practitioners to acquire and implement job related knowledge and skills in their classrooms (see the next section, *Practitioners*).

In the Palm Beach QIS, professional development is part of a center's overall star rating, counting for 20% of a program's final star rating. All practitioners employed at the center are included in the professional development assessment and scoring. The education level of practitioners and the Annual 50 Points on professional development (intended to encourage practitioners to pursue continuous improvement activities that support professional development beyond the 10 hour annual in-service licensing requirement) are used to determine the professional development/staff qualification star rating of the center. Specifically, the star rating is calculated as the percentage of practitioners achieving specified education levels (i.e., staff qualification) and the Annual 50 Points score. To promote continuous improvement, the percentage of practitioners required to attain specific education levels increases as a center moves upward on the star ratings. Requirements for staff education levels and Annual 50 Points at each star level are presented in Appendix 4A.

Other pathways to quality in the Palm Beach QIS are staff-to-child ratio and group size, program, and curriculum (star ratings for these pathways to quality are presented in Appendix 4A). The Palm Beach QIS prescribes smaller group size for greater child initiations, more opportunities to extend language, deeper mediation of children's social interactions, and stronger supports for exploration and problem solving (see NAEYC, 2006). Programs with lower staff to child ratio are in a better position to individualize experiences based on the needs of children and provide appropriate care, stimulating learning activities, and a safe environment. This pathway counts for 10% of a program's final star rating.

Another pathway is a program consisting of family engagement and administration, and it counts for 15% of a program's final star rating (7.5% for family engagement and administration, respectively). The logic behind family engagement is that programs that effectively involve families are more likely to meet the needs of children. Therefore, quality programs recognize the primacy of children's families and establish respectful relationships with children's families to support and promote children's optimal learning and development (see NAEYC, 2006). The Palm Beach QIS promotes a variety of ways as an ongoing process for families to get involved with early childhood education such as meetings between parents and practitioners, family events, and newsletters. The purpose of the administration pathway is to measure leadership and management in early childhood education. Overall, administrative practices are crucial to ensure and sustain high quality interactions and learning environments at the classroom level.

The Palm Beach QIS requires all programs to choose a developmentally appropriate curriculum approved by the Early Learning Coalition. The Coalition offers a list of curricula from which programs can select, or programs can submit their curricula to the Coalition for approval. The Palm Beach QIS uses three environment rating subscales to assess a program's developmentally appropriate practice: listening and talking, activities, and program structure in ITERS or language reasoning, activities, and program structure in ECERS. The average classroom score for these subscales is used to determine the quality of this pathway counting for 15% of a program's final star rating.

To some extent, these pathways to quality in the Palm Beach QIS allude to the matrix model of system design (for local QIS). These pathways clearly target practitioners, centers (administration), children, and parents (family). Although standards are not explicitly established in the Palm Beach QIS, it is obvious that many design features in the Palm Beach QIS have the capability to address and fulfill standards. We can appreciate this point more in the following discussion on other components in the matrix model of system design.

Practitioners

The key point to develop this component in the matrix model of system design is to find ways to equip practitioners with abilities to accomplish prescribed standards for early childhood education. The Palm Beach QIS has a simple solution which may well be the best solution to this task: get practitioners trained. Training does not simply mean taking courses in the Palm Beach QIS. Quality support, another major component in the Palm Beach QIS, is a series of programs and incentives. Nevertheless, all of them have the same goal to get practitioners trained so as to improve their job related knowledge on content and pedagogy.

Early Learning Coaches Program is one of the most valuable services in the Palm Beach QIS. Early learning coaching is an evidence based mentoring practice designed on the basis of the eight stages of the consultation process in Buysse and Wesley (2004). They provide a framework for the change process in early childhood settings. This dynamic process engages practitioners in a collaborative working relationship with coaches aimed to promote positive change. With knowledge on the stages of consultation, coaches and practitioners form a firm foundation to achieve shared goals for positive change. This idea to pair practitioners with experienced coaches to create training mentorship is innovative. Specifically, certified teachers employed by the School District of Palm Beach County provide on-site technical assistance to help practitioners resolve difficulties and challenges in their classroom practices. Early learning coaches go through specialized training in quality improvement and consultation process. They spend time getting to know the centers and their programs and building relationships with practitioners (and administrators). Early learning coaches then work with practitioners to develop and implement plans for quality improvement that focus on the pathways to quality.

Career Advisors Program provides a critical service in the Palm Beach QIS. Each center receives guidance and advisement from an assigned career advisor employed by the Institute of Excellence in Early Care and Education located in the Palm Beach State College. The advisor works with practitioners (and the administrator) to develop a center professional development plan that focuses on the professional development pathway. The advisor also works one on one with practitioners employed at the center for career advisement. A private, confidential setting is provided for individual advising sessions at the center, at the Institute of Excellence, or at other agreed upon locations. With the help of the advisor, practitioners develop an individual development plan that identifies education and training that can advance them along a career pathway. Depending on the career goals of practitioners, the advisor assists them in selecting formal education (for credit) or informal training (without credit).

Professional Development Opportunities Program is available through formal education and informal training. Courses (for formal education) and workshops (for informal training) are designed and developed using the Florida Core Competencies for Early Care and Education Practitioners. This document identifies essential knowledge and skills that practitioners need to implement high quality programs and services that support children and their families. Courses and workshops are designed to support the development of competencies among practitioners in seven core knowledge areas:

- Health, safety, and nutrition;
- Child development and learning;
- Building family and community relationships;
- Teaching and learning environments and interactions;
- Curriculum;
- Observing, documenting, screening, and assessing to support young children and their families;
- Professionalism.

Practitioners pursue education and training in these core knowledge areas through two pathways. One pathway allows them to accumulate college credits; the other pathway earns them no college credits. Nevertheless, core competencies are embedded in both pathways to provide a link between them. This link enables practitioners to transition between pathways with minimum effort as they strengthen their early childhood classroom practices.

SEEK (Seeking Excellence in Education and Knowledge) Scholarship Incentive Award provides monetary awards to practitioners who complete specific education or training requirements. Two award programs recognize practitioners as they achieve specific education or training benchmarks, including the Education Incentive Award (EIA) and the Informal Training Incentive Award (ITIA). The awards are distributed annually and require applications within designated time periods.

Childcare WAGE$ Florida Salary Supplement Program is designed to assist administrators of childcare facilities to retain practitioners by rewarding educational achievement and longevity. The WAGE$ program is fully funded by the Children's Services Council of Palm Beach County and administered through the Institute of Excellence in Early Care and Education. It provides education based wage supplements to early childhood practitioners working directly with children from birth to five years of age. WAGE$ supplements are based on the level of education already attained and continued employment at a center. Payments are distributed in six month increments after practitioners have been employed for one year in the same center. Career advisors provide practitioners with applications and supplemental information on the program.

Translation and Evaluation of Foreign College Degrees are provided by the Palm Beach QIS. This convenient service is available for foreign nationals who have been employed at the same program for six months and have completed the 45 hour Department of Children and Families certification. Career advisors work with these practitioners to use this year-round service. Translation and evaluation of foreign college degrees through regular channels are a very tedious and time-consuming process. This thoughtful service is really a "signature" feature of the Palm Beach QIS.

Palm Beach County Early Childhood Registry serves the local early care and education community in many ways:

- Elevating the status of the profession,
- Aiding in planning education and training opportunities,
- Raising public awareness about the critical importance of quality early childhood care and education.

As a means to document and acknowledge education, training, and professional achievements of practitioners working within the field of early childhood care and education, a registry is common to professional development systems and generally addresses aspects of both practitioners and trainers. The Palm Beach County Early Childhood Registry maintains a database that provides a system for collecting, storing, and reporting data about the early childhood education field which supports ongoing community planning for professional development efforts and initiatives. The registry has several components:

- *Training calendar* maintains a comprehensive list of registry approved training events for the early care and education workforce offered by various registry approved trainers or training organizations;
- *Trainer (training) approval* establishes standards and criteria for evaluating training materials, verifies core knowledge areas, and promotes quality of training;
- *Storage* maintains records and documentations on professional development, provides information for career advising, and determines future education and career goals;
- *Practitioner achievement and recognition* recognizes professional achievements of practitioners, providing a psychological "paycheck" to practitioners who have been committed to career pathways and professional development.

The registry plays an important role in the Palm Beach QIS. Membership in the registry is a requirement for all QIS practitioners. In fact, it is expected that all practitioners are members of the registry prior to acceptance of application. Professional development achievement that is not documented in the registry prior to assessment is not counted in the assessment of the professional development pathway.

The registry provides both trainer and practitioner reports to registry members through secure personal login. Registry reports include formal and informal professional development accomplishments as well as licensing requirement trainings. All training must be at least two hours in length and award 0.2 Continuing Education Units (CEU) in order to be accepted for entry on the registry report. In order for the registry report to display the most current information, registry members are asked to continuously update the registry as professional development accomplishments are achieved. For QIS centers, keeping the registry report updated and complete is essential because the information contained in the registry is used to conduct the assessment of the professional development pathway.

There are two types of training listed on the registry report. Registry approved quality assurance (QA) includes trainings that have gone through the registry training approval system. These trainings are reviewed by quality assurance coordinators to ensure that they align with the early childhood content areas established by the State of Florida. Also included in this category is the online training offered by the Florida Department of Children and Families and the Florida Department of Education. Registry approved not quality assurance (Not QA) includes trainings that have not gone through the registry training approval process but are from agencies that are recognized to provide high quality training (e.g., accredited institutions of higher education). There are also secondary training options that do not weigh as much as the above training options but do count toward benchmarks or requirement of professional development pathway. Some examples are:

- Registry approved conferences (e.g., Children Count Conference, NAEYC annual conference)
- College credit courses not in the area of early child care and education (e.g., foundations of education, college geometry)
- Training events not in the area of early child care and education (e.g., case management, standards for quality afterschool programs)
- College preparation courses
- General education (high school) training

Meanwhile, the Palm Beach QIS also acknowledges registry verified trainings that have neither gone through the registry training approval process nor are from approved training organizations (e.g., accredited institutions of higher education). Although these trainings are recorded on the registry report if completed during the past 2 years, they do not count toward benchmarks or requirements of professional development pathway.

Finally, the Palm Beach QIS allows what is referred to as center trainer option in recognition that administrators are a great resource for training practitioners. Administrators have the option to provide up to 15 hours of registry approved training per assessment cycle to practitioners working in their centers, provided they meet all requirements established to become registry approved center trainers who must hold a valid Department of Children and Families Early Childhood Staff Credential and complete a course on the foundations of outcomes driven training. The trainer may either submit training materials for registry approval or use the Center Trainer Manuals developed by the Institute of Excellence in Early Care and Education and approved by the registry. The Center Trainer Manuals are multimedia trainings which include a training script, materials for activities and exercises, and an observation tool that helps transfer what has been learned in the training to the classroom.

Centers

Administrators (i.e., directors or owners) of childcare facilities play a very important role in the fulfillment of standards for early childhood education. The matrix model of system design contains this critical component. The key to the design of this component is twofold. We need to train administrators to become effective leaders and assist them to overcome challenges in their work. The Palm Beach QIS designed a series of programs and incentives to help administrators develop personal leadership skills and manage their centers effectively. We have discussed some of these programs and incentives including administration as one of the pathways to quality as well as the programs (or incentives) of WAGE$ and Quality Enhancement Payments. There are other programs and incentives designed to improve leadership quality in the Palm Beach QIS.

Accreditation Support is part of the assignment of an early learning coach who provides accreditation support for a center that needs to go through the accreditation or reaccreditation process. Support is individualized, based on the needs of the center. The early learning coach works collaboratively with the administrator throughout the whole process. This support is in addition to the services provided by the assigned early learning coach.

Career Advisors Program also applies to administrators. The advisor visits each center to work jointly with the administrator (and practitioners) to develop a center professional development plan. The goal is for the administrator to gain an understanding of the professional development pathway so as to guide practitioners toward a mutually agreed upon outcome. Many factors can affect the plan such as staff turnover as well as education and training achievements attained by practitioners. The advisor works with the administrator to review and revise the plan regularly.

Personal and Professional Development Course is for administrators (and practitioners) who desire to lead professional development and who aspire to continuous improvement (pursue continuous learning). Palm Beach State College designs and offers this course for the purpose of sustaining professional development.

Roadmap to Quality Counts is a systematic effort that helps administrators navigate the Palm Beach QIS. This 12 hour training series gives administrators an overview of the Palm Beach QIS in terms of its history, purposes, benefits (to children and community), pathways, assessments, and available resources. Administrators actively engage in learning more about ways to apply quality care to their centers and to improve their classroom practices. The course is divided into multiple sessions. Sessions include guest speakers and partners involved in the Palm Beach QIS. Topics deal with pathway standards for early childhood environment, curriculum and instruction, ratio and group size, and professional development. Attendance to all sessions is required for administrators to earn 1.2 CEU.

Mini Grants Program is a one-time opportunity to help centers pay for some of the costs associated with doing routine business at a higher quality level (i.e., improving quality). A center is eligible for up to $5,000 based on its benchmarks, timelines, and expenditures (see Table 4.1). The amount of a mini grant is also related to the size of the center and the number of full time practitioners (i.e., staff to child ratio). A program may build up its mini-grant dollars by delaying receipt of the grant. Accumulating mini-grant dollars may be beneficial for a center if the administrator and the early learning coach have targeted a major purchase to assist with quality improvement. For example, if a program needs child size furniture and purchase of that furniture exceeds the amount of the first distribution amount, the program may hold onto its three-month grant allocation. This amount can be added to either or both of the six-and nine-month allocations, respectively. However, because mini-grant money is only meant to supplement expenditures, a program may choose to make other purchases in a timelier fashion. If extra time is needed to meet benchmarks, the early learning coach may extend the mini-grant opportunity up to 18 months, depending on the progress on benchmarks. Capital improvements cannot be funded with mini-grant dollars. Should a program choose to withdraw from QIS and re-apply later on, the program is not eligible to receive additional mini-grant money.

Table 4.1: *Distribution of Mini Grants*

Count of Full Time Equivalent Children	Annual amount of Mini Grant
Less than 50	\$2,000
Between 51 and 100	\$3,000
Between 101 and 150	\$4,000
More than 151	\$5,000

Quality Enhancement Payments are designed to help with the costs associated with providing quality care and education that go beyond basic licensing requirements. Payments are provided for centers that meet or exceed the three star level (minimal standards) at gradually increasing rates. Children's Services Council requires centers to utilize these payments to support continued quality improvement activities such as:

- Staff retention (e.g., wage enhancements, employee benefits),
- Professional development,
- Allocation of funds for substitute practitioners,
- Purchase of developmentally appropriate materials for use by children in care,
- Technology upgrades.

Quality Enhancement Payments come from public funding. To ensure that the payments are used appropriately, designated staff from the Children's Services Council visit centers throughout the year to review documentations regarding the spending of the payments. The Palm Beach QIS uses the following guidelines to assess payments (see also Table 4.2):

- Quality Enhancement Payments are based on the overall star rating and FTE (full time equivalent) attendance counts (excluding school aged children),
- A program's overall star rating is based on the weighting of pathways,
- A program is eligible for quality enhancement payments for star ratings of 3 stars and above,
- A program's attendance count is based on the sign-in and sign-out sheets from the same weeks that the School District of Palm Beach County selects for its October and February FTE counts,
- Administrators must submit copies of sign-in and sign-out sheets within five days of completed assessment:
  - If a center is assessed during the months of November through February, the October sign-in and sign-out sheets are used
  - If a center is assessed during the months of March through October, the February sign-in and sign-out sheets are used
- Quality enhancement payments are distributed on a quarterly basis and are prorated based on the date of the assessment,
- Quality enhancement payments can only be made to those programs that have current enrollment and attendance,
- Quality enhancement payments are used for the sole purpose of improving programs such as educational materials, technology upgrades, professional development, wage enhancement, and employee benefits. Supporting documentation on the use of funds must be provided upon request. Misuse of quality enhancement payments subjects a center to termination.

Table 4.2. *Distribution of Quality Enhancement Payments*

Attendance Counts of Children	3-Star Level	4-Star Level	5-Star Level
Less than 50	$12,000	$18,000	$21,000
Between 51 and 100	$14,000	$20,000	$23,000
Between 101 and 150	$16,000	$22,000	$25,000
More than 151	$18,000	$24,000	$27,000

Director Portal is a tool that is designed for administrators to use as a valuable resource to assist in managing their participation in the Palm Beach QIS. Administrators can use the portal to access their centers' assessment reports, star ratings, professional development plans, and registry records, both past and current. There is also an email feature in the portal that allows administrators to communicate with early learning coaches and career advisors. Administrators need only a computer with internet access, and the Palm Beach QIS assigns user names and passwords for them to access the portal. Training sessions are provided for administrators to use the portal, and technicians are available for any technical difficulties with the portal (e.g., log-in problems, loss of user names or passwords).

Pathway Checklists help administrators plan, implement, monitor, and revisit quality improvement activities. Some pathways to quality are straight forward; others including family engagement, administration, and curriculum require comprehensive and systematic planning to reach a higher star level, because each of them is of multifaceted efforts. The Palm Beach QIS has designed checklists for administrators to manage these pathways easily and effectively (see Appendices 4B, 4C, and 4D). Similarly, to make star ratings transparent and understandable, the Palm Beach QIS has also designed a scoring guide to share with administrators (see Appendix 4E). Referred by some administrators as "cheat sheets," these checklists and scoring guide have proven to be very useful administrative tools to work with QIS.

Children

As practitioners and administrators strive to meet high quality standards for early childhood education, learning outcomes of children are expected to raise. The component of children in the matrix model of system design therefore emphasizes measuring, assessing, and monitoring children's learning outcomes. It is indeed a good idea to consider this component as a monitoring system for dual purposes. One purpose is to track children's learning progress; the other is to provide curricular and instructional feedback for practitioners and administrators to adjust and improve their classroom practices. We provide a list of highly recognized instruments for the purpose of measuring, assessing, and monitoring children's learning outcomes.

- Bracken Basic Concept Scales (BBCS) is a developmentally sensitive measure of children's basic concept acquisition and receptive language skills.
- Clinical Evaluation of Language Fundamentals Preschool-2 (CELF PreK-2) provides a variety of subtests to comprehensively test the language

skills of preschool-aged children who will be in an academic-oriented setting.

- Concepts About Print (CAP) is an assessment of emergent literacy print concepts.
- Developmental Indicators for the Assessment of Learning (DIAL) is an early childhood screener of early childhood development in both English and Spanish.
- Dynamic Indicators of Basic Early Literacy Skills (DIBELS) is a set of procedures and measures for assessing the acquisition of early literacy skills, designed to be short (one minute) fluency measures that can be used to regularly monitor the development of early literacy and early reading skills.
- Expressive One-Word Picture Vocabulary Test (EOWPVT) is an individually administered, norm-referenced assessment of how well younger children can name objects, actions, or concepts presented in full-color pictures.
- Hawaii State Readiness Assessment (HSRA) is an assessment of kindergarten readiness based on professional observation and judgment of kindergarten teachers who observe children according to behaviors, concepts, or skills identified in various developmental domains.
- Peabody Picture Vocabulary Test (PPVT) is an untimed test of the receptive vocabulary of children and provides a quick estimate of their verbal ability or scholastic aptitude.
- Phonological Awareness Literacy Screening PreK (PALS-PreK) is a scientifically-based phonological awareness and literacy screening that measures preschoolers' developing knowledge of important literacy fundamentals that are predictive of future reading success.
- Preschool and Kindergarten Behavior Scales (PKBS) is a behavior checklist administered to parents to identify social skills and problem behaviors of children.
- Preschool Comprehensive Test of Phonological Processing (Pre-CTOPP) assesses phonological awareness, phonological memory, and rapid naming among young children.
- Test of Language Development (TOLD) is one of the most widely used tests of spoken language that identifies oral language proficiency in children.
- Woodcock-Johnson Diagnostic Reading Battery (WJDRB) is an individually administered diagnostic test that assesses phonological awareness, phonics knowledge, reading achievement, and related oral language abilities.

Parents

When we think about the establishment and fulfillment of standards for early childhood education, it is so easy to leave parents out of the equation. Yet parents have long been a critical part of education reforms. For example, parental choice is a powerful means for accountability of education systems. The bottom line for parents to be able to make any contribution to an education system is to be informed of their children' education quality and educated about options and resources that they can apply to demand positive educational change. The component of parents in the matrix model of system design applies exactly the same principle: get parents informed and educated.

The Palm Beach QIS also relies on the same principle to design parental involvement. We discussed earlier family engagement as one of the pathways to quality where through engagement parents get informed and educated of the Palm Beach QIS and how they can assist to make the effort successful. Apart from that, the main approach taken by the Palm Beach QIS to work with parents is consumer education.

Consumer Education Opportunities Program serves three main purposes:

- Inform parents about centers' participation in and children's involvement with QIS,
- Explain high quality standards to parents,
- Help parents realize, expect, and seek out high quality in their children's care and education.

Some Critical Issues

In the rest of the chapter, we briefly discuss some common but critical issues embedded in the matrix model of system design. Each QIS designed based on any design model addresses these issues either implicitly or explicitly.

Feedback. QIS, as an operational system, needs to evolve constantly as it strives to be more effective and more efficient in improving quality of early childhood care and education. The most important mechanism to facilitate positive change (adjustment) of any QIS is feedback. Specifically, the operation of any QIS generates large amount of data on standards, practitioners, centers, children, and parents. These data are the basis for feedback. Data driven decision making becomes thus critically important in the process of generating credible feedback. For many years, the Palm Beach QIS has used external researchers to perform independent program evaluations to generate feedback to improve the operation of QIS (i.e., data driven decision making). External evaluations have focused on outcomes as a result of participation in QIS concerning practitioners, centers, and children. In fact, several chapters of this book report the results of these evaluations. The experience of the Palm Beach QIS suggests that external researchers are a valuable approach to monitor and inform the operation of QIS. One recommendation for future external evaluations of QIS is to link outcomes of practitioners, centers, children, and parents with standards for early childhood education more explicitly so that external feedback eventually becomes standards specific for improvement and advancement.

Technology. All major standards for formal education (e.g., mathematics education) advocate for and even push teachers to pursue the use of technology in classroom practices. We believe that technology can also benefit early childhood education. Nevertheless, we remind practitioners and administrators in early childhood settings that technology must be introduced to young children in an age appropriate manner to avoid potential harm. For example, watching screens excessively may harm young children. In fact, we suggest that the use of technology should be brief and infrequent. Young children are in a developmental stage in which they learn more naturally from the exploration of concrete materials (e.g., blocks) to discover relationships. In contrast, the exploration of relationships via analyzing images on computer screens is actually too abstract for young children to discover meaningful relationships. We realize that issues such as this may use more clinical and psychological studies to be certain, but we believe that caution is definitely necessary when designing QIS that involves large scale technology interventions.

Grass Roots. This issue is simple and straightforward yet easy to ignore and challenging to implement. We refer to grass roots as people who have direct, close relationships with children. These are practitioners and parents. It is common for committees or task forces to rightfully involve experts in child development, specialists in school subjects, and stakeholders in the design of QIS. Nevertheless, practitioners and parents are the ones who contextually know what their children are capable of achieving and what can be realistically done in their classrooms. The achievable yet challenging principle of NAEYC applies well to the design of QIS, and we believe that this principle cannot be fruitful until we involve grass roots in the design of QIS.

References

Buysse, V., & Wesley, P. W. (2004). A framework for understanding the consultation process: Stage-by-stage. *Young Exceptional Children*, 7(2), 2–9.

Child Care Bureau. (2006). *Table 6—Child Care and Development Fund Preliminary Estimates: Average Monthly Percentages of Children Served in All Types of Care (FFY 2005). FFY 2005 CCDF Data Tables (Preliminary Estimates).* Washington, DC: Administration on Children, Youth and Families. U.S. Department of Health and Human Services.

CTB/McGraw-Hill. (2003). *Pre-kindergarten standards: Guidelines for teaching and learning.* Retrieved from http://www.home.earthlink.net/~sagesolutions/PreKstandards.pdf

Head Start Resource Center. (2011). *The Head Start child development and early learning framework: Promoting positive outcomes in early childhood programs serving children 3–5 years old.* Arlington, VA: Author.

National Association for the Education of Young Children. (2008). *Early childhood program standards and accreditation criteria.* Washington, DC & Arlington, VA: Author.

National Association for the Education of Young Children. (2006). *Standards for early childhood professional preperation programs. A position statement.* Washington, DC & Arlington, VA: Author. Retrieved from http://www.naeyc.org/file/naeyc/file/positions/ProfPrepStandards09.pdf

National Council of Teachers of Mathematics. (1991). *Professional standards for teaching mathematics.* Alexandria, VA: Author.

Scott-Little, C., Kagan, S. L., & Frelow, V. S. (2003).*Standards for preschool children's learning and development: Who has the standards, how were they developed, and how were they used?* Greensboro, NC: Regional Educational Laboratory at SERVE.

Virginia Department of Education. (2010). *K-3 mathematics achievement records.* Richmond, VA: Author. Retrieved from http://www.doe.virginia.gov/instruction/mathematics/elementary/K-3_math_achievement_records.shtml

Appendix 4A: *Pathways to Quality Standards for Child Care Centers and School Based Sites*

Learning Environment (40%)				
Instruments: Early Childhood Environment Rating Scale (ECERS) and Infant/Toddler Environment Rating Scale (ITERS) Subscales: Space Furnishings, Personal Care Routines, Language Reasoning, Activities, Interaction, Program Structure Scale: 1 = Inadequate, 3 = Minimal, 5 = Good, 7 = Excellent Scoring: Average score of sample of classrooms.				
Star Rating				
1	2	3	4	5
ECERS 3.00 – 3.49	ECERS 3.50 – 3.99	ECERS 4.00 – 4.49	ECERS 4.50 – 5.49	ECERS 5.50 – 7.00
ITERS 3.00 – 3.49	ITERS 3.50 – 3.99	ITERS 4.00 – 4.49	ITERS 4.50 – 5.49	ITERS 5.50 – 7.00

Staff Qualification and Professional Development (20%)

Star Rating				
1	2	3	4	5
All staff have enrolled in the 40-hour DCF training within 90 days of hire 40 hours certification completed within one year of hire 5-hour Early Literacy completed 1 staff per 20 enrolled children have DCF Staff Credential Facility Director holds level I or II Director Credential	Associate Teachers: 25% have HS diploma/GED, 25% have DCF EC Staff Credential, 25% have one 3 credit ECE class or 45 hours informal ECE training annually, if higher benchmarks are not met. Lead Teachers: All have HS diploma/GED, 75% have DCF EC Staff Credential and 75% have one 3 credit ECE class or 45 hours informal ECE training annually, if higher benchmarks are not met. Facility Director has HS diploma/GED, DCF EC Staff Credential and one 3 credit ECE class or 45 hours informal ECE training annually, if higher benchmarks are not met	Associate Teachers: 50% have HS diploma/GED, 50% have DCF EC Staff Credential, 50% have one 3 credit ECE class or 45 hours informal ECE training annually, if higher benchmarks are not met. Lead Teachers: All have HS diploma/GED, 90% have DCF EC Staff Credential and 90% have one 3 credit ECE class or 45 hours informal ECE training annually, if higher benchmarks are not met. Facility Director has HS diploma/GED, DCF EC Staff Credential or and one 3 credit ECE class or 45 hours informal ECE training annually, if higher benchmarks are not met	Associate Teachers: 75% have HS diploma/GED, 75% have DCF EC Staff Credential, 75% have one 3 credit ECE class or 45 hours informal ECE training annually, if higher benchmarks are not met. Lead Teachers: All have HS diploma/GED, DCF EC Staff Credential, 90% have one 3 credit ECE class or 45 hours informal ECE training annually, if higher benchmarks are not met. 25% have completed 12 ECE credit hours 25% will hold an Associate degree or higher with 12 ECE credits or 60 credits with 12 ECE credits Facility Director has HS diploma/GED, DCF EC Staff Credential, completed 12 ECE credit hours, and holds FL Advanced level credential Associate degree or higher with 12 ECE credits or 60 credits with 12 ECE credits	Associate Teachers: All have HS diploma/GED, DCF EC Staff Credential, 75% have one 3 credit ECE class or 45 hours informal ECE training annually if higher benchmarks are not met and 25% have completed 12 ECE credit hours Lead Teachers: All have: HS diploma/GED, DCF EC Staff Credential, and completed 12 ECE credit hours, if higher benchmarks are not met. 50% will hold an Associate degree or higher with 12 ECE credits or 60 credits with 12 ECE credits Facility Director has HS diploma/GED, DCF EC Staff Credential, completed 12 ECE credit hours, and holds FL Advanced level credential Associate degree or higher with 12 ECE credits or 60 credits with 12 ECE credits
10 hour State In-service Requirement	25% Professional Staff completed annual 50 points	50% Professional Staff completed annual 50 points	75% Professional Staff completed annual 50 points	100% Professional Staff completed annual 50 points

Staff to Child Ratio and Group Size (10%)

	Star Rating									
	1		2		3		4		5	
Age	Ratio	Group	Ratio	Group	Ratio	Group	Ratio	Group	Ratio	Group
Infant	1:4	n/a	1:4	12	1:4	8	1:4	8	1:4	8
1	1:6	n/a	1:6	12	1:6	12	1:5	10	1:5	10
2	1:11	n/a	1:9	18	1:8	16	1:7	14	1:6	12
3	1:15	n/a	1:13	26	1:12	24	1:10	20	1:9	18
4 and 5	1:20	n/a	1:16	32	1:13	26	1:10	20	1:10	20

Program (15%)

Star Rating				
Family Engagement (7.5%)				
1	2	3	4	5
Family Handbook is written and includes parental rights and responsibilities Signed acknowledgement of receipt of handbook by parent	Minimum of 3 modes of communication are used to share child and program information with families	At least 2 family activities per year provided	Families are invited to scheduled family-teacher conferences to review child's progress and needs and to set goals. 2x/year Activities provided for children and families to assist with transition to new settings within the child care program and/or to kindergarten	Families have opportunity to evaluate the provider in writing at least annually Resources are available to communicate with families in the family's primary language Activity suggestions are developed with staff and families for children identified with delays
Administration (7.5%)				
Risk management plan is in place (written action plan for emergencies such as hurricanes, fire, flood, etc. including evacuation routes identified and practice drills)	Personnel policy manual includes written staff orientation procedures and job descriptions Staff Turnover Reports submitted to Registry monthly	Staff meetings are held at least quarterly Written performance evaluations are completed annually	Written operating policies & procedures include standard business and fiscal management practices Marketing plan is in place to maximize full enrollment Performance evaluations include classroom observation	Salary scale is in place and is differentiated by education, experience Financial recordkeeping system provides quarterly reports and analysis and 1 year projected budget Performance evaluations include professional development plans

Curriculum (15%)

Star Rating				
1	2	3	4	5
Compliance with the Early Learning Coalition of Palm Beach County's service agreement process for curriculum implementation. Curriculum is on Coalition's list OR program has successfully completed Coalition review process.	On the applicable Environment Rating Scales, the program has achieved average scores of 3.50 – 3.99 (Level 2) on the following subscales: Activities, Language Reasoning (ECERS) or Listening and Talking (ITERS), and Program Structure.	On the applicable Environment Rating Scales, the program has achieved average scores of 4.00 – 4.49 (Level 3) on the following subscales: Activities, Language Reasoning (ECERS) or Listening and Talking (ITERS), and Program Structure.	On the applicable Environment Rating Scales, the program has achieved average scores of 4.50 – 4.99 (Level 4) on the following subscales: Activities, Language Reasoning (ECERS) or Listening and Talking (ITERS), and Program Structure.	On the applicable Environment Rating Scales, the program has achieved average scores of 5+ (Level 5) on the following subscales: Activities, Language Reasoning (ECERS) or Listening and Talking (ITERS), and Program Structure.
On the applicable Environment Rating Scales, the program has achieved average scores of 3.00 – 3.49 (Level 1) on the following subscales: Activities, Language Reasoning (ECERS) or Listening and Talking (ITERS), and Program Structure.			Written lesson plans for developmentally appropriate curriculum (see 6 weeks of past lesson plans) that highlight curriculum area for ages birth to five.	A system is in place for ongoing child observations, individualized program planning and family communication. Process of completing ongoing child observations at least three times per year is described in writing (may be in the personnel policies and/or the family handbook). Samples of child observation form, anecdotal notes, and/or child portfolios that reflect goals and progress for each individual child observed for at least 30% of children enrolled (names deleted) Evidence that progress is shared with families.
				Child assessment guides individualized program planning and communicating with families. Lesson planning forms in use include a section for activities targeted towards meeting identified needs of individual children.

Appendix 4B: *Family Engagement Checklist*

1 Star	Family Handbook is written and includes all of the following (Please highlight areas in handbook and indicate page numbers):
	____ Schedule of operations
	        ____ Daily opening-closing hours
	        ____ List of holidays
	____ Payment policies regarding
	        ____ Payment due dates
	        ____ Fees for late pick-up, if any
	____ Nutrition policies and procedure regarding
	        ____ Food provided by the center
	        ____ Food brought from home, if any
	        ____ Allergy precautions
	____ Illness policy
	____ Medication policy
	____ Emergency procedures: procedure for notifying families in the case of an emergency (i.e., power outage, hurricane, injured child, etc)
	____ Signed acknowledgement of receipt of handbook (upon enrollment or annually). 100% of current children enrolled are expected to have a signed acknowledgement. 10% of files will be randomly checked by the Assessor

2 Star	A minimum of 3 modes of communication are used to share child and program information with families. Documentation may be classroom specific or center based. At least 3 items below must be checked. ____ Daily or weekly individual written reports for children (2 different samples, can be blank) ____ Newsletters (4 examples) ____ Letters, flyers, or invitations announcing projects or events (2 examples) ____ Bulletin board designed to share information with families. Must be current information and all areas listed below must be observed during the on-site data collection visit. ____Health ____Parent information ____Community involvement ____Log of informal communications for assessment period (phone, email, written notes) ____Monthly calendar (lunch or snack menu, center events or classroom events)

3 Star	At least 2 different family activities are provided per year. Documentation for items below can be in the form of a sign-in sheet, announcement, or photos. Documentation may be classroom specific or center based. Name of activity and date must be included. At least 2 items below must be checked. ____ Open house ____ Holiday celebration ____ Volunteer or center based service activities ____ Family classroom participation ____ Field trips designed for families ____ Group family meetings ____ Classes for families such as positive discipline, nutrition, etc ____ Lending library ____ Family or child journaling activities

4 Star	Families are invited to schedule family-teacher conferences to review child's progress and needs, and to set goals, twice a year. ____ Policy stating families are offered 2 conference opportunities twice a year ____ Sample conference summary report form that includes goals, parent signature, and staff signatures Activities are provided for children and families to assist with transition to new settings within the child care program and/or to kindergarten. ____ Written description of procedures for transitioning a child from one group to another ____ Evidence of transition activities (can include a transition schedule, photos, letter to families).

5 Star	Families have an opportunity to evaluate the provider in writing at least annually _____ 10% of completed surveys _____ Summary of completed surveys Resources are available to communicate with families in the family's primary language _____ Written list of primary languages spoken by families currently enrolled Requirements for families who *do not* communicate in English: (can be NA) _____ Plan of communication for each language spoken: contact information of adult interpreter _____ Written communications (at least 1 per language) of any kind are provided in all languages identified as primary language of families Activity suggestions are developed with staff and families for children identified with delays _____Copies of activity suggestions provided by specialists/program staff for any child diagnosed with a disability (child has IFSP or IEP), are developed in collaboration with families. Documented examples can be found on site

Appendix 4C: *Administration Checklist*

Appendix 4C

Administration Checklist

1 Star	Risk Management Plan Action steps for emergencies per Health Department Requirements ____ Fire ____ Severe Weather Risk management plan and system that includes documentation of: ____ Posted Evacuation Plans in each classroom ____ Monthly Evacuation Drills (fire drill logs will be verified) ____ Annual review of the Risk Management Plan and emergency procedures (dated staff meeting agenda or minutes)

2 Star	Personnel Policy and Procedures Manual: The program's Personnel Policy and Procedures manual should be included in the Quality Counts Binder. For this section, highlight areas in the manual or indicate the page number on which the item can be found Job descriptions for all positions at the site. Mark NA for those positions that do not apply. ____Director ____Floater ____Assistant Director ____Curriculum Specialist ____Lead Teacher ____Other ____Associate Teacher Staff orientation must include at least 8 of the following: ____Center philosophy and goals ____Attendance policy ____Staff training requirements ____Ethical conduct policy ____Resignation or termination policy ____Child abuse and neglect reporting procedures ____Health and safety procedures ____Discipline policy for staff ____Insurance (health, life, dental, vision, etc.) ____Retirement and/or annuity plan ____Child care discount for staff ____Tuition reimbursement ____Paid leave time ____Paid time for professional development Staff turnover ____Monthly Staff Turnover Reports submitted to Palm Beach State College Early Childhood Registry during assessment year

3 Star	Staff Meetings _____Dated agendas and sign-in sheets to document that meetings are held at least quarterly Annual Performance Evaluations _____Written performance evaluations signed by employees and an administrator for all teaching staff employed for at least one year

4 Star	Operating Policies and Procedures ____Health and safety procedures (optional for 2 star, required for 4 star) ____Hiring procedures ____Organizational chart Marketing Plan ____Written action steps for ____Recruiting families with children, ____Providing visibility in the community ____Advertising Documentation of a Marketing Plan must include at least 4 of the following (actual items or photos of items must be placed into the Administration binder). ____Public relations tools (ads, newsletters, letterhead stationery, business cards) ____Promotional items (clothing, mugs, pens, etc.) ____Professional, consistently-used logo ____Signage ____A referral rewards program ____Partnership with businesses ____Membership in a Chamber of Commerce ____Advisory Board or other staff meeting minutes that show a review of recommendations for the marketing plan Annual Performance Observation ____Written performance evaluations include observation by an administrator for all teaching staff employed for at least one year

5 Star	Salary Scale ____Written salary scale is used, showing differentiation by job title, education or experience Financial Reports and Budget (checked on site) ____Quarterly financial statements (4) or 1 annual statement for the last fiscal year (can be in the form of a bank statement reconciliation or a profit and loss statement) ____Current or projected budget

Appendix 4D: *Curriculum Checklist*

1 Star	On the applicable Environment Rating Scale, the center has achieved average score of 3.00 – 3.49 on the following subscales: Activities, Language Reasoning (ECERS) or Listening and Talking (ITERS), and Program Structure. If the average score is below 3.00, zero points will be awarded for the Curriculum Pathway Developmentally Appropriate Curriculum ____Copy/evidence of approved curriculum
2 Star	On the applicable Environment Rating Scale, the center has achieved average score of 3.50 – 3.99 on the following subscales: Activities, Language Reasoning (ECERS) or Listening and Talking (ITERS), and Program Structure.
3 Star	On the applicable Environment Rating Scale, the center has achieved average score of 4.00 – 4.49 on the following subscales: Activities, Language Reasoning (ECERS) or Listening and Talking (ITERS), and Program Structure.
4 Star	On the applicable Environment Rating Scale, the center has achieved average score of 4.50 – 4.99 on the following subscales: Activities, Language Reasoning (ECERS) or Listening and Talking (ITERS), and Program Structure. Developmentally appropriate curriculum and lesson plans for ages birth to five ____Lesson plans, for each classroom, for the 6 weeks prior to the assessment period

5 Star	On the applicable Environment Rating Scale, the center has achieved average score of 5.00+ on the following subscales: Activities, Language Reasoning (ECERS) or Listening and Talking (ITERS), and Program Structure. A system is in place for ongoing child observations ____Process of completing ongoing child observations at least 3 times a year is described in writing ____Child observation form, anecdotal notes, or child portfolios observed for at least 30% of current children enrolled Child assessment guides individualized program planning and communicating with families ____Lesson planning form must include space for individualization. For example, J.R. (or Johnny, or Child 7) will pick a song to sing during transition from outside to the bathroom)

Appendix 4E: *Final Star Rating Form*

Appendix 4E
Final Star Rating Form

Assessment Date:						
Site Name:						
Pathway	Score		Star Rating	x Weight	Equals Total Points	Bonus Points
Learning Environment (40%)	ITERS			2		Bonus Points: 1 or 2 Bonus Points will be given to centers based on the percentage of professional staff with a Bachelor's degree in Early Childhood Education/Child Development. • At least 25% = 1 Bonus Point • 50% or more = 2 Bonus Points
	ECERS			2		
	*ITERS OR ECERS Only			4		
Staff Qualifications and Professional Development (20%)		Star Rating		2		
	Staff Qualifications					
	Annual 50 Points					
	Lower of 2 Star Rating Scores					
Staff to Child Ratio and Group Size (10%)				1		
Curriculum (15%)				1.5		1 Bonus Point will be given to centers if they have a designated Curriculum Specialist with a Bachelor's degree and a minimum of 12 credits in ECE who oversees a center's educational program for at least 50% of the time.
Program Operations (15%)	Family Engagement			0.75		
	Administration			0.75		
Final Star Rating Points:						Bonus Point Designation:
43.00 – 50.00 points = 5 star rating			Subtotal			
37.00 – 42.99 points = 4 star rating						2 bonus points for 50% or more and one bonus point for designated curriculum specialist
25.00 – 36.99 points = 3 star rating			Bonus Points			
13.00 – 24.99 points = 2 star rating			Total Points Earned			
4.00 – 12.99 points = 1 star rating			Gold Seal Designation			
Star Rating+: Programs holding a Gold Seal designation will earn a star rating "plus".			Final Star Rating			

5

The Implementation of the Quality Improvement System

XIN MA, JIANPING SHEN, IN COLLABORATION WITH CHILDREN'S SERVICES COUNCIL OF PALM BEACH COUNTY, EARLY LEARNING COALITION, INC. OF PALM BEACH COUNTY, FAMILY CENTRAL, INC., PALM BEACH STATE COLLEGE INSTITUTE OF EXCELLENCE, AND THE SCHOOL DISTRICT OF PALM BEACH COUNTY

Quality improvement system (QIS) is a comprehensive, voluntary effort that seeks to enhance the quality of early childhood care and education for very young children often from birth to age five. The key words in this statement from the perspective of implementation are "comprehensive" and "voluntary." These key words imply key principles for the implementation of any QIS design. In this chapter, we will illustrate these principles, coupled with experiences from the Palm Beach QIS. Our goal is to streamline an implementation mechanism with a clear benchmark for each principle for self-evaluation by individuals or agencies in charge of QIS.

Convincing Administrators and Practitioners

Because of the voluntary nature of QIS, both administrators and practitioners of early child care and education centers need to be convinced of the benefits of participation in QIS for child development in general and for centers and practitioners specifically. Perhaps, advertisement is the most effective approach to make known the benefits for participation. Advertisement can be placed in local or state newsletters or websites of professional organizations associated with early childcare and education. Direct mailings to administrators and practitioners introducing QIS can be very effective. Articles in local or state newspapers can also carry the message in an influential way. It is always critical to leave a phone number for administrators and practitioners to pursue any further inquiry. Real people rather than automated messages are always important to provide immediate explanations and clarifications that can greatly encourage participation.

QIS may need to have its own website that functions to provide detail that other media approaches cannot afford. For example, sufficient research evidence can be made available in the QIS website. Public stories and personal testimonies from past and current QIS can also be featured. In addition, local, state, and national advocacy groups can play an important role in getting the message out, and one should not underestimate the role of parents. These efforts help convince administrators and practitioners that QIS is worthy of their participation.

The Palm Beach QIS strongly emphasizes the benefits of participation for administrators. It allows an administrator to set the course for the level of quality in a program. Specifically, the administrator sets goals for improvement in every aspect of the program (i.e., practitioners, children, and families). It can be very challenging for administrators to achieve and maintain high quality in areas of early care and education on one hand and on the other hand manage and operate the business aspects of a program. The Palm Beach QIS offers invaluable resources and supports for administrators who choose to participate, including

- Program standards to help administrators identify and target areas of improvement
- On-site technical assistance to support quality improvement efforts
- On-site career advising for practitioners
- Scholarships for practitioners to achieve center professional development goals
- Financial incentives that help administrators to retain practitioners
- Training (continuing education) opportunities for administrators and practitioners
- Mini-grants for centers
- Funding to support center quality improvement
- Marketing materials for administrators
- Use of a program's star rating as an effective marketing tool
- Networking opportunities for administrators and practitioners
- Access to the Director's Portal for administrators
- Consumer education opportunities for center parents

We have discussed all these initiatives in detail in Chapter 4 where the design of local QIS is our focus. Furthermore, the Palm Beach QIS conveys a number of benefits for early childhood care and education programs that centers offer. The fundamental benefit is all the knowledge (i.e., all the knowhow) to improve the quality of their programs, emphasizing that children they serve are able to enter schools ready and eager to learn.

The benchmark for this principle of implementation is that administrators and practitioners are convinced of the benefits of participation in QIS. They become informed or aware of the existence of QIS, balance pros and cons of participation, appreciate all resources and supports to be made available for them, and determine the benefits associated with participation worthy of the challenges.

Providing Clear Expectations for Participation

Educational reforms are serious social pursuits. Coming with the benefits of participation are expectations to strive for improvement to meet pre-established standards. Expectations for administrators and practitioners must be presented as challenging yet achievable. That QIS is challenging speaks to the fact that serious commitments and efforts are required in educational reforms, and struggles and difficulties should be expected in every aspect of educational change. That QIS is achievable speaks to the determination to make as many resources and supports available as administrators and practitioners need to overcome all challenges. Participation in QIS enters administrators and practitioners into a contract with accountability. The fear on the part of administrators and practitioners is that agencies in charge may play "hardball" with them. The Palm Beach QIS wants to ensure administrators and practitioners that agencies in charge, referred to as QIS partners in the Palm Beach QIS, have standards in their work with local administrators and practitioners.

The Palm Beach QIS includes as (operation) partners Children's Services Council, Early Learning Coalition, Inc., Family Central, Inc., Palm Beach State College Institute of Excellence, School District of Palm Beach County, and Children's Forum. These partners are expected to use quality standards to help administrators and practitioners determine their programs' needs for improvement and to provide assistance in the development of an improvement plan for each program. Other expectations include:

- Supporting the quality improvement efforts of programs by working closely with administrators and practitioners to set achievable benchmarks and timelines,
- Following through with administrators and practitioners on all mutually agreed commitments,
- Conducting themselves in an ethical and professional manner at all times,
- Respecting a program's ownership of the quality improvement work.

A program participating in the Palm Beach QIS is expected to commit to continuous quality improvement at all levels of the organization and is responsible for making necessary changes to enhance the quality of the program. Indeed, a program's commitment to continuous improvement is the key to success and upward progress through QIS. The annual program agreement used in the Palm Beach QIS is presented in Appendix 5A.

The benchmark for this principle of implementation is that administrators and practitioners are clear about what is expected of them for participation in QIS. They should demonstrate confidence that with resources and supports to be made available to them they are able to meet all of the expectations. Administrators and practitioners should also feel ensured of a fair evaluation of their programs and efforts.

Reinforcing Expectations with Accountability

To some extent, expectations may not be necessarily binding. In contrast, accountability holds outcomes of expectations responsible. Accountability for participation in QIS should include at the very least two aspects. One is that the minimum standards for improvement in early childhood care and education must be achieved as a condition for continuing QIS funding; the other is that the use of QIS funding (in particular public funding) must be subject to local, state, and federal laws. To reinforce expectations with accountability for participation, we emphasize applications as confirmations of commitments. A formal application brings in accountability, with its approval indicating willing and serious commitment and compliance of an applicant to all professional and financial standards. The Palm Beach QIS treats application for QIS seriously with a careful, multistep procedure. Each step can serve as a benchmark for this principle of implementation.

Step 1. Attend orientation and training. All programs that desire to participate in the Palm Beach QIS are invited to attend an orientation overview that explains the goals, improvement processes, and supports that are available upon acceptance. There is a more detailed training after the orientation, open for enrollment to administrators and practitioners of programs that are interested in participation as well as newly accepted or already actively involved programs. This training gives participants an overview of the purposes, pathway requirements, and available resources. The Palm Beach QIS uses its website to announce periodical orientations and trainings and commissions one of the QIS partners, Family Central, to conduct orientations and trainings.

Step 2. Application. Interested, licensed programs that receive public funding for child care must meet prerequisite and entry requirements (see Appendices 5B and 5C) and complete an application (see Appendix 5A). Applications can be accessed and submitted online on an ongoing basis throughout the year. These are good features of convenience for administrators who are willing to participate.

Step 3. Application review and selection. Depending on the amount of available public funding (i.e., system capacity), the Palm Beach QIS accepts approximately 20 to 30 programs annually which include centers, school based sites, Head Start or Early Head Start sites, and family childcare homes. A committee reviews all applications. Programs are informed of the status of their applications within 30 days of submission. Selected applicants are placed in a queue. As the system becomes able to take in additional programs, applicants are notified of their participation. The committee uses the same aforementioned prerequisite and entry criteria to make decisions (see Appendices 5B and 5C).

Step 4. Liaison visit. Once a program has been accepted, the center is contacted to schedule an appointment for the administrator (sometimes a board member) to meet with the designated partners of the Palm Beach QIS. The purpose of this visit is to ensure that there is a clear understanding of the level of commitments and expectations and to answer any questions that the administrator may have about the Palm Beach QIS.

Making Preparations for Participation

Coming along with centers entering QIS is the essential step of planning for interventions or making preparations for participation. A combination of self-assessment and external evaluation to identify the needs of a center for quality improvement may prove to be the most ideal. This approach combines the realistic reflection of self-assessment with the empirical vigor of external evaluation. When such an ideal approach is not practical for various reasons, expert evaluation on the needs of a center for quality improvement is a good alternative. It is in fact one of the steps in the implementation of the Palm Beach QIS. We intend to demonstrate the entire implementation process of the Palm Beach QIS by using its original sequential steps across the sections (principles) of this chapter.

Step 5. Introductory visits by early learning coach and career advisor. Within 30 days of acceptance into the Palm Beach QIS, programs are contacted to schedule introductory visits by the assigned early learning coach and career advisor. As we have discussed in Chapter 4, one of the main roles of an early learning coach and career advisor is to help a center identify areas in need of quality improvement and develop a center plan for quality improvement. The early learning coaches and career advisorss are experts in this context to evaluate a center with the administrator and practitioners for the purpose of designing perhaps the most critical task for QIS—the plan for action. This task highlights the importance of training early learning coaches and career advisors on theories of educational change and evaluation because success or failure of a center in effort to improve early childcare and education quality largely resides on this plan. The benchmark for this principle of implementation is a plan of action that is targeted, challenging, and achievable.

Thinking Sequentially

Given the comprehensive nature of QIS, it is unthinkable that the overall QIS plan for quality improvement is one gigantic leap forward. Granted, no programs of a complex nature can make a giant leap and succeed. Instead, success usually consists of small but sure leaps. Therefore, it is a necessary measure for implementation that one thinks of QIS sequentially. The Palm Beach QIS demonstrates this wisdom with three phases of implementation of interventions (intensive phase, maintenance phase, and self-directed phase).

Step 6. Intensive phase. The 18-month intensive phase begins from acceptance into the Palm Beach QIS. This is a collaborative process where parameters are established, and reasonable goals and target dates are set based on the priorities of the administrator of a center. Specifically, for the first 18 months, the program receives intensive, on-site early learning coaching. The early learning coach and the administrator jointly produce an achievable program improvement plan with benchmarks and target dates based on the strengths and challenges identified in the assessment. Professional development plans for practitioners may also be produced. The early learning coach meets with the administrator regularly. The ultimate goal for this phase is to prepare the administrator to gain all the necessary knowledge to become self-sufficient so as to implement and sustain quality improvements as the center moves on to the maintenance phase. As can be seen, building relationships is an integral part of this phase as early learning coaches, administrators, and practitioners work together to improve early childcare and education quality of their centers.

The benchmark for this principle of implementation is that gradual, sequential phases are specified with a concrete plan of quality improvement for each phase. The assessment procedure should also be in place (as a benchmark) to measure and evaluate outcomes of quality improvement in each phase.

Communicating Effectively

In the context of comprehensive, voluntary educational reforms such as QIS, effective communication is critical. Voluntary administrators and practitioners are usually eager to communicate with QIS partners because they have strong desires to change. Regular communications between QIS partners and administrators and practitioners with meaningful programmatic information help centers effectively adjust their course (plan) of actions for change. The Palm Beach QIS produces an annual assessment report for each center using the Environmental Rating Scale (ERS, as we discussed in Chapter 4) and other programmatic information to help the administrator measure progress in and identify factors relevant to his or her initial concern for change. In addition, the Palm Beach QIS uses early learning coaches and career advisors as bridges of communications as they regularly visit centers to work with administrators and practitioners on early childcare and education quality improvement. The benchmarks for this principle of implementation are the channels, scales, and frequencies of communications between QIS partners and administrators and practitioners.

Monitoring Regularly

As we just argued, meaningful programmatic information makes communication between QIS partners and administrators and practitioners effective because credible data drive changes effectively. Meaningful programmatic information, nevertheless, comes from monitoring the progress of a center regularly in order to provide meaningful feedback to the administrator and practitioners. The Palm Beach QIS attempts to provide meaningful feedback to administrators and practitioners on its most important component, various pathways to quality. An overall star rating of a program measuring combined quality of pathways is also provided to each center.

Step 7. Pathway assessments. The process of pathway assessments consists of care and learning environment star rating based on the most recent annual ERS assessment score and annual assessment of the remainder of the pathways (i.e., staff qualification and professional development, staff to child ratio and group size, curriculum, and program including family engagement and administration).

Step 8. Star rating. Programs receive their first star rating after the completion of the assessment following the 18-month intensive phase. In other words, upon the completion of the annual assessment, programs receive an overall star rating for early childcare and education quality.

Monitoring must be a continuing or ongoing process throughout the implementation of any QIS, with the same purpose of providing regular, meaningful programmatic information to aid adjustment over a center's plan of actions. The Palm Beach QIS continues its regular monitoring efforts beyond the intensive phase.

Step 9. Maintenance phase. After 18 months in the Palm Beach QIS (i.e., the intensive phase), a program enters the maintenance phase which includes setting further target dates for continued quality improvement in all pathways to quality, with limited onsite technical assistance from an early learning coach. In this phase, administrators assume main responsibility for maintaining and sustaining quality in their centers. With some support from their early learning coaches, administrators are responsible for establishing desired, achievable benchmarks, implementing a center improvement plan, and developing classroom activity records. Early learning coaches now function as consultants to help administrators make quality improvement to their programs. They schedule monthly appointments to provide consulting support to administrators and monitor target dates to ensure that a program continues to make progress towards quality improvement.

Step 10. Self-directed phase. A program enters the self-directed phase, the last phase of coaching, when it achieves a level of early childcare and education quality that no longer calls for regular on-site coaching and consultation. The administrator and the early learning coach make this determination together for a program, considering several factors such as the length of time in the system, the achieved goals of the program, the maintenance of the progress, and the consistency in the level of early childcare and education quality provided (as indicated by star rating). Once a program is seen to have attained and sustained all its quality goals, it is referred to as a model program that can be copied after by other programs (e.g., newly entered ones). Nevertheless, the administrator and the early learning coach are still loosely coupled. The early learning coach may schedule quarterly visits with the administrator, or the administrator may contact the early learning coach by phone or through the Director's Portal as needed.

The benchmark for this principle of implementation is the mechanism that allows ongoing monitoring of the progress made by centers in QIS. The mechanism should have sufficient functions to collect, analyze, and interpret quantitative and qualitative data as well as provide meaningful programmatic feedback to centers. In the maintenance and self-directed phases, this mechanism is particularly critical due to the reduced interactions between centers and QIS. Administrators and practitioners depend very much on meaningful programmatic feedback to sustain quality improvement.

Forming a Learning Community

We intend to introduce Wenger's (1998) notion of community of practice in the context of QIS. When administrators, practitioners, early learning coaches, and career advisors are given the opportunity to learn from one another, they form what Wenger (1998) refers to as a community of practice defined as "shared histories of learning" with a focus on learning as social participation (p. 86). A comprehensive educational reform such as QIS represents a great opportunity for administrators and practitioners to reflect upon and rethink about their early childcare and education practices. Wenger(1998) refers to this interaction as the "urgent need for reflection and rethinking" (p. 9). He described three dimensions that characterize the community of practice. These dimensions are good benchmarks for this principle of implementation.

The first dimension is mutual engagement that involves administrators, practitioners, early learning coaches, and career advisors working together and negotiating meanings with one another about early childcare and education. In QIS, this process can effectively take place in formal meetings involving early learning coaches and career advisors, through email discussions, and even informally in the staff lunch rooms as administrators and practitioners discover, develop, define, and establish evolving forms of mutual engagement aimed at quality improvement on early childcare and education.

The second dimension is a joint enterprise that involves administrators, practitioners, early learning coaches, and career advisors negotiating the meanings and vocabularies tied to a given improvement task or activity. In QIS, usually administrators and practitioners carry out the joint task of implementing a center improvement plan and thus should hold one another accountable by discussing, reflecting, and critiquing on the outcome of every issue or component on the improvement plan.

The third dimension is a shared repertoire that involves a wide variety of things from routines to tools. In QIS, administrators, practitioners, early learning coaches, and career advisors can use their experiences learned from various QIS initiatives to renegotiate meanings that define what a classroom or environment with quality early childcare and education should look like when implementing the improvement plan. According to Wenger (1998), constant renegotiation exists within the community of practice. QIS should offer administrators and practitioners plenty of opportunities to participate in such a community of practice in which the meaning of effective early childcare and education is being constantly renegotiated.

From our experiences working with and researching through existing QIS systems in the country, we are disappointed to notice that very few QIS efforts involve, or may even be aware of, community of practice. We believe that any QIS should actively encourage the establishment of community of practice. After all, community of practice is one of the best ways to promote sustainable professional development for administrators and practitioners. The educational philosophy of QIS takes root easily and firmly within community of practice. There is no requirement on the size of a community as long as meaningful interchanges are evident and sufficient among members of the community. There can be a community within each center or across centers. Special technical assistance such as early learning coaches and career advisors in the Palm Beach QIS can become a critical leading voice in community of practice. For example, early learning coaches and career advisors can greatly help and facilitate the establishment of community of practices within and across centers.

Dealing with the Unexpected

In a comprehensive educational reform such as QIS that involves a large number of early childcare and education centers, unexpected circumstances are bound to happen. If unprepared, these circumstances can create great difficulties and disturbances in the implementation of QIS. It is important for QIS to foresee potential problems that are likely to happen during the implementation stage. New QIS efforts can learn a great deal about these potential problems from existing QIS efforts. The benchmark for this principle of implementation is the foresight and preparation for the unexpected, with detailed procedures, measures, and strategies in place to cope with the unexpected. To some extent, the Palm Beach QIS provides valuable experiences in preparing for the unexpected.

Hiatus Policy. According to the Palm Beach QIS, a hiatus is the most common problem that creates challenges in the implementation of QIS initiatives. The Palm Beach QIS has developed hiatus policy for centers facing unusual circumstances. If a childcare and education program does not have children enrolled for a period of three consecutive months, the program is put on hiatus. Requests for a hiatus are handled on a case-by-case basis. Requests from programs could be granted up to 90 days. While on hiatus programs do not receive the support of early learning coaches or quality enhancement payments (see Chapter 4 for details). If a program still has no children attending after its hiatus of up to 90 days, the program is terminated from QIS. The program, however, is given priority status for re-entry into QIS if enrollment improves later on. Administrators who do not have children enrolled in their programs due to seasonally scheduled closing of their facilities are not affected by this policy.

New Owner Policy. In the event that a new owner takes over an existing QIS center, the following procedure is established in the Palm Beach QIS:

- A liaison visit and meeting are scheduled with the new owner,
- The new owner writes a letter of intent to continue in QIS within one month of the new license,
- The center is offered limited technical assistance from an early learning coach for one year,
- Practitioners continue to receive support for professional development including career advising and financial incentives,
- Quality enhancement payments cease.

During the year, the new owner is required to complete all of the following benchmarks:

- Register for and attend orientation and training for administrators,
- Maintain compliance with licensing standards (i.e., without notice of violations),
- Maintain compliance with all applicable agreements with QIS.

After the new owner has been in operation for one year, the following procedure applies:

- The center completes the application process,
- If accepted, the center begins intensive coaching for 18 months,
- The center becomes eligible for mini-grants and other incentives.

Finally, in the case of acquisition through inheritance of an early childcare and education center that is enrolled in QIS, the status of the center in QIS is considered a special case and determined by the Palm Beach QIS leadership.

New Employee Policy. The Palm Beach QIS requires that all practitioners must be active in the Palm Beach State College Registry. Newly employed practitioners at existing QIS centers who are not active registry members must complete, sign, and submit the registry practitioner application with supporting documentation to the registry and become an active registry member within 30 days from the date of hire. Practitioners who are not active are still assessed for the professional development pathway, which could have negative implications to the professional development star rating.

Compliance Policy. As a tool for programs to get back on track in order to remain in QIS, a compliance plan is developed for programs that do not adhere to QIS policies and agreements in the Palm Beach QIS. Grounds for a compliance plan for a program include:

- One Class 2 violation in 12 consecutive months, or
- Citation for having a recurring licensing violation in a period of three consecutive months (i.e., Class 3 violation), or
- Quality improvement is not maintained and must be consistently readdressed by the early learning coach and the career advisor.

Violation of any part of the QIS annual agreement may result in either a compliance plan or an immediate termination depending on the severity of the violation and the history of the compliance. When a program is in need of a compliance plan, the following procedure for its development and implementation is established in the Palm Beach QIS:

- Appropriate QIS partner meets with the administrator of the program to explain the process and reasons for a compliance plan,
- The administrator and the partner agree to enter a compliance plan,
- The administrator and the partner create a plan of compliance which includes specific measurable benchmarks,
- The partner follows up in 30 days to determine the next steps with the administrator,
- All benchmarks in a compliance plan must be met within 90 days to avoid a possible termination from QIS.

Exit Policy. The Palm Beach QIS reserves the right to take any action necessary for the betterment of the system. Termination can be initiated at any time based on the recommendations of QIS partners. Meanwhile, administrators may also request to exit QIS at any time. Grounds for an immediate termination of a QIS center include:

- One Class 1 violation at any time, or
- Two Class 2 violations within 12 consecutive months, or
- More than one compliance plan within a year, or
- The administrator fails to meet benchmarks by the target dates set in a compliance plan, or
- The administrator refuses to enter into a compliance plan.

The procedure for a center to exit the Palm Beach QIS is:

- If the administrator initiates the exit, he or she submits a notification in writing to the Palm Beach QIS,
- If QIS initiates the exit, QIS partners meet with the administrator to explain the exit process and conduct an exit interview,
- The administrator receives a letter stating the reason for exiting, the effective date, and the benefits that need to be forfeited.

Exit from QIS results in the termination of all services. Practitioners enrolled in courses and workshops at the time of termination are able to complete their current training work. When conditions improve, administrators are allowed to apply to re-join QIS, but their centers must meet all current prerequisites before re-applying to QIS.

Conducting Assessment

Assessment of the outcomes is an integral part of QIS. One naturally thinks of children when the word, assessment, appears. We have discussed the assessment of children in terms of instruments in Chapter 4. We intend to discuss more on this issue now from the perspective of implementation. After the centerpieces of QIS are designed and implemented, assessment is needed to examine each and every centerpiece as it produces outcomes. In the case of the Palm Beach QIS, assessment centers around the pathways to quality, the centerpieces of the Palm Beach QIS. Because this chapter focuses on implementation, we intend to discuss the procedural implementation of assessment (on the pathways) to accompany our discussion on the nature of the pathways in Chapter 4.

Learning Environment. The Palm Beach QIS performs assessment in one day or over several days within a three week assessment window. One third of the total classrooms is assessed at each center with a minimum of two classrooms. At least one classroom in which the majority of children are younger than 30 months and at least one classroom in which the majority of children are older than 30 months are randomly chosen to be assessed. The assessor uses the Infant/Toddler Environment Rating Scale (ITERS) to assess the classrooms with younger children and the Early Childhood Environment Rating Scale (ECERS) to assess the classrooms with older children. A program's average ITERS and/or ECERS classroom score becomes the pathway score for learning environment (see Appendix 4A).

Assessment reflects a typical day in the classroom. Administrators inform assessors when they arrive if there is anything atypical in each of the classrooms on that day. Quality usually exhibits consistently every day, and thus assessment generally takes place unless there is a new practitioner or a new substitute. Assessors determine if the assessment would continue if there is a new practitioner or a new substitute. There is no informal assessment, and all assessments count towards quality scores. Only practitioners who are typically present in the classroom are permitted to remain in the room during any assessment.

Staff Qualification and Professional Development. All practitioners who are employed at a center are included in the assessment of this pathway. The level of practitioner education (staff qualification) and annual 50 points (professional development) for all practitioners at the center are reviewed to determine the star rating on this pathway. The star rating is based on the percentage of practitioners achieving specified educational levels and the annual 50 points earned on professional development.The percentage of practitioners required to attain specific levels of education increases as a program moves up the star rating scale.

The process for scoring staff qualification is to average star ratings of all categories of practitioners (lead practitioners and various associate practitioners). Each category receives a star rating based on professional development benchmarks. The minimum percentages required to meet a star rating level are presented in Appendix 5D (see also Appendix 4A). In order to reach a star rating level, each benchmark must meet the minimum percentage. The star rating for each category is averaged by adding the star ratings and dividing by the total number of job titles at the center. To score professional development, the 50 annual points are calculated based on the percentage of all practitioners as one group. Finally, the lower of the staff qualification score and the 50 annual points score becomes the star rating for this pathway.

Staff to Child Ratio and Group Size. The Palm Beach QIS collects ratio and size information from its ERS assessments to determine a score for this pathway. The procedure includes the following steps:

- The assessor conducts a staff to child ratio and group size observation on all the classrooms serving children from birth to five years of age during the annual ERS assessment visit,
- The assessor records the number of practitioners and the number of children present in each classroom (see Appendix 5E),
- The administrator signs off on the record documentation,
- The assessor uses this information in conjunction with birthdates provided by the administrator and most recent classroom roster to calculate averages on ratio and size as the star rating for this pathway (see Appendix 4A).

Program. This pathway contains two parts: family engagement and administration. Assessment takes the form of checklist on each component (see Appendices 4B and 4C). In addition, the Palm Beach QIS emphasizes a critical aspect of the program: monthly staff turnover. Turnover data provide insight to administrators and QIS partners concerning the longevity of employment in the early childcare and education workforce and help create and implement new strategies and initiatives to encourage practitioners to remain employed at their centers. Turnover information can also encourage administrators to evaluate employee satisfaction in the workplace. Tracking practitioner turnover is a function of the registry. The process is to have center administrators complete and submit a report on monthly staff turnover. The Palm Beach QIS allows either paper or electronic submissions (see Appendix 5F).

Curriculum. The Palm Beach QIS assesses this pathway in the following steps:

- Three ERS subscales are used to report on a program's developmentally appropriate practices,
  - language reasoning, activities, and program structure in ECERS
  - listening and talking, activities, and program structure in ITERS
  - scores for these subscales are listed on the annual assessment report and the average classroom score for these subscales is used in part to determine this pathway (see Appendix 4A)
- The pathway checklist is a guideline that includes the standards and documentation requirements for each star level (see Appendix 4D),
- The center provides documentation for items at each star level in order to achieve that level and move on to the next level,
- The assessor reviews documentation on site during the annual assessment visit. Programs are not allowed to submit documentation after the visit.

Overall Star Rating. The pathways are assessed by reviewing documentation gathered by administrators as well as information collected from other data sources such as documentation maintained by QIS partners. The administrator of each center prepares a box of binders or file folders containing documents for review, clearly labeled for easy access and review by the assessor. Documents on the pathways to quality are checked either during the three week assessment window or at a later date appropriate to the assessor. Everything must be available on the day of the document check. The Palm Beach QIS considers certain items not necessary to be placed in any binder (i.e., curriculum books; child observation forms, anecdotal notes, and child portfolios; emergency phone numbers posted in each classroom; evacuation maps posted in each classroom; bulletin board concerning health, parent information, and community involvement; signed acknowledgment of receipt of handbook). The assessor verifies compliance for certain items on the administration, curriculum, and professional development pathways using data provided by administrators and QIS partners. Each center is responsible for the compliance with these items.

A star rating ranging from 1 star to 5 stars is assigned to each pathway. Each pathway is also assigned a weight (derived from percentages in Appendix 4A). When the star rating is multiplied by the weight of the pathway, the result is measured in points (see Appendix 4E). Points for each pathway are tallied (referred to as the subtotal points), and any bonus points that a program may have earned are added to determine the total points earned, ranging from 4.00 to 50.00. The total points earned for a program translate into the final star rating for the program.

It is possible to achieve up to three bonus points. One or two bonus points, depending on the percentage of practitioners who meet the requirement, are awarded to programs in which practitioners have earned a bachelor's degree in early childhood education or child development. Specifically, one bonus point is earned if a quarter of all practitioners have earned the degree, whereas two bonus points are earned if at least half of all practitioners have earned the degree. Another bonus point is awarded to programs that have a designated curriculum specialist who has a bachelor's degree and a minimum of 12 credits in ECE (early childhood education) and who oversees a center's educational program with duties equal to 0.5 FTE.

Finally, programs that hold a Gold Seal designation earn a star rating plus to highlight their accreditation status. The assessor verifies Gold Seal status via the information contained in the website of the Department of Children and Families to determine which sites have earned the Gold Seal designation.

Reference

Wenger, E. (1998). *Communities of practice: Learning, meaning and identity.* New York: Cambridge University Press.

Appendix 5A: *Palm Beach QIS Annual Program Application/Agreement*

Palm Beach QIS Annual Program Application/Agreement

Section 1: Program Information (Please Print)

Program Name and Type (Center, Family Child Care, Head Start, School Based)			License Number
Corporate Name			Email Address
Address	City	State	Zip
Owner			Phone
Director and length of time in position			Fax
Is Your Program Accredited? If so, by whom?			Is Program Exempt from Licensing?
If licensed, How long has this program been licensed by current owner?		Service Agreement: Yes ______ No ______	
Licensed Capacity ______	Current Enrollment (Birth-5 yrs) ______	Num. of Subsidized Children: (Birth-5 yrs) ______	Hours of operation ______ AM to ______ PM

Please list number and type of classrooms by age groups: (Example: 1- Infant class, 4- two year old classes, VPK and or Head Start/Early Head Start, etc.)

If admitted into Quality Counts, We (on behalf of ______________________________) will agree to the following: Legal entity or business name if not incorporated

1. As Director/Owner/ Board Chairperson, we understand that our facility **must maintain** its licensure status and compliance with licensing standards, have held a valid license for a year and **be in compliance with all applicable agreements (e.g., service agreement, VPK).**
2. We agree to provide access to Quality Counts: Environment Rating Scale assessment results, accurate and up to date information on staff development, staffing patterns, family engagement and program administration.
3. We will allow program access to an Early Learning Coach for the purpose of providing technical assistance to the Director and/or staff as needed.
4. We agree to fully cooperate and create improvement plan(s) with our Early Learning Coach that set benchmarks and we agree to meet those benchmarks that demonstrate program improvement within agreed time frames.
5. We understand that licensing violations, non compliance with service/VPK agreements and/or failure to meet improvement benchmarks within agreed time frames are subject to compliance plans and/or termination from Quality Counts.
6. We understand that providing fraudulent or inaccurate information is subject to termination from Quality Counts.
7. We agree to fully cooperate and support the creation of professional development plan(s) for the program and individual staff members with a Career Advisor and to support staff's efforts to attend trainings, classes and workshops to the fullest extent possible.
8. We agree to have 100% staff membership in the Early Childhood Registry (Director and all staff) and to include new staff within 30 days of employment.
9. We understand that the purpose of Quality Counts is to enhance quality in child care settings to improve child outcomes and that we may be eligible for quality enhancement payments if we attain a 3-Star rating or above.
10. We understand that participation in Quality Counts and our program's star rating is public information.
11. We agree to submit to Quality Counts sign in and out sheets for FTE counts in order to process Quality Enhancement Payments. Failure to submit could result in nonpayment.
12. We agree to use Quality Enhancement payments for the **sole purpose** of improving the program: Staff retention, wage enhancement/employee benefits, establishment of a budget to support staff professional development including an allocation of dollars for substitute teachers, purchase of developmentally appropriate materials for use by the children in care and technology upgrades. We agree to provide supporting documentation/physical proof of Quality Enhancement payment expenditures. Misuse of Quality Enhancement payments is subject to termination from Quality Counts and reimbursement to Quality Counts for all misused payments. In the event of any litigation arising under this Agreement, the prevailing party shall be entitled to reasonable costs including attorney's fees, at the trial, appellate and post- judgment levels. The venue of any such litigation shall be had only in the courts of Palm Beach County, Florida.
13. We understand that if there is a change in Owner and/or Director we will notify Quality Counts Manager/Family Central Inc. in writing, within two weeks of change.
14. We understand in order to access updated information and manage our participation in Quality Counts, a computer and internet connection is necessary.
15. We attest that all information included in the application is true and accurate.

Section 2: Annual Agreement

***Signature of Owner (if unincorporated) or President/Board Chairperson (if incorporated)**		
Printed Name	**Title**	**Date**
***Signature of Program Director**		**Date**

***Owner and Director must sign this application.**

Section 3: Staff Credentials/Education

Site Name:

- List all professional staff employed at your site. Run off additional sheets if needed. Please write site name on each sheet.
- Check the boxes above credentials and/or degrees held by each staff member. Form must be filled out completely.
- Please Note: All professional staff listed below are required to be active members of the Palm Beach County Early Childhood Registry with DCF transcript and all educational diplomas and transcripts submitted. **Registry reports for all staff listed below must be included with your application paperwork. Registry reports must contain all credentials/education checked below. Failure to meet this requirement will automatically disqualify this Quality Counts application.** For more information on the PBC Early Childhood Registry including how to print your Registry report or how to become a member, please visit www.pbcregistry.org

List all **professional** staff *

F=Full Time

(Works 20 or more hours per week)

P=Part Time

(Works less than 20 hours per week)

Name:

First

Last

F or P

Professional Staff

D=Director

AD=Assistant Director

LT=Lead Teacher

AT=Associate Teacher

ES=Education (Curriculum) Specialists

Age Group of Class Assignment

Primary Language Spoken

E=English

S=Spanish

C=Creole

O=Other

Employment Start Date

Credentials/Education (Please complete all items that apply)

HS =High School Diploma **GED** = Valid Diploma Credential

40 + 5 DCF = 40 Hour Introductory DCF Certification, plus 5 Hour Literacy

Staff Cred = Current and Valid Staff Credential issued by DCF

Dir. Cred = Current and Valid Director Credential issued by DCF

CCC = Completion of a Florida Department of Education Certified College Credit Certificate Program in Early Childhood Education

AA/AS = Associate Degree **BA/BS** = Bachelor's Degree

MA/MS = Master's Degree **PhD** = Doctorate Degree

TCC = Total Number of College Credits Completed

EC = Number of College Credits in Early Childhood Completed

(Check/Complete all that apply)

Example:		X					No	X						X	X		X		X	X			156	12
Susan Brown	F	D	AD	LT	AI	E3	Classes	E	S	C	O	1/01/2011	HS	GED	40 + 5 DCF	Staff Cred	Dir Cred	CCC	AA/ AS	BA/BS	MA/MS	PhD	TCC	EC
Example:				X					X				X		X	X							3	3
Maria Gomez	P	D	AD	LT	AT	ES	Infants	E	S	C	O	3/15/2002	HS	GED	40 + 5 DCF	Staff Cred	Dir Cred	CCC	AA/ AS	BA/BS	MA/MS	PhD	TCC	EC
		D	AD	LT	AT	ES		E	S	C	O		HS	GED	40 + 5 DCF	Staff Cred	Dir Cred	CCC	AA/ AS	BA/BS	MA/MS	PhD	TCC	EC
		D	AD	LT	AT	ES		E	S	C	O		HS	GED	40 + 5 DCF	Staff Cred	Dir Cred	CCC	AA/ AS	BA/BS	MA/MS	PhD	TCC	EC

Appendix 5B: *Palm Beach QIS Prerequisites Checklist*

A Program Must Meet All Criteria

____Has the program been licensed for at least one year?

____Has the program received no class I violations within the last 24 months **or** if licensed less than 24 months, during the period of operation?

____Has the program received fewer than 2 class II violations within the last 24 months **or** if licensed less than 24 months, during the time period of operation?

____Does the program receive public funding (such as Head Start, subsidized, VPK)?

____Is the program in compliance with its agreements (service agreement, VPK)?

____ All professional staff employed at the site are required to be active members of the Palm Beach County Early Childhood Registry with DCF transcript and all educational diplomas and transcripts submitted.

Appendix 5C: *Palm Beach QIS Entry Scoring Criteria*

Item	0	1	2	3	4	5
Zip Codes Served	All other zip codes	N/A	N/A	N/A	N/A	33401, 33403, 33404, 33405, 33406, 33407, 33408, 33409, 33415, 33417, 33430, 33438, 33460, 33461, 33462, 33476 and 33493
Health Department Violations	N/A	One class II violations (regardless of class III) in the past 24 months. No more than 3 unsatisfactory Licensing reports, one year prior to application date-present	No class II violations and no more than 5 class III violations within the past 24 months. No more than 2 unsatisfactory Licensing reports, 1 year prior to application date-present.	No class II violations and 2-5 class III violations within the past 24 months. No more than 1 unsatisfactory Licensing reports, one year prior to application date-present.	No class II violations and no more than 1 class III violation within the past 24 months. No unsatisfactory Licensing reports, one year prior to application date-present	No violations of any kind within the past 24 months.
Percentage of subsidized children	Less than 10%	10 % +	20% +	30% +	40% +	50% +
Program serves infants and (/or) toddlers	No	N/A	N/A	The program serves infants or toddlers	N/A	The program serves both infants and toddlers
Program Operation Same Owner/Director	1 year	1 - 2 years	2 - 3 years	3 - 4 years	4 - 5 years	5 years or more
Accreditation (aligned with Gold Seal)	Program is not accredited	Program is accredited 1 year	Program is accredited 2 years	Program is accredited 3 years	Program is accredited 4 years	Program is accredited 5 years or more
Mission/Vision	The site has neither a Vision nor Mission Statement	N/A	N/A	N/A	N/A	The Program has either a Vision or Mission Statement
Training Policy	The program does not have a written training policy	N/A	N/A	The written policy outlines the minimum training required by licensing	N/A	The written policy exceeds minimum training required by licensing
QC Orientation	No orientation	N/A	N/A	QC Orientation	N/A	Roadmaps to Quality Counts Training

Appendix 5D: *Palm Beach QIS Form on Benchmarks/Staff Qualifications*

1-Star☐	QC Benchmarks and Staff Qualifications	2-Star ☐			3-Star ☐			4-Star ☐			5-Star ☐		
Licensing Standards **For Teaching Staff and Facility Director**		*Assoc. Tacher	Lead Teacher	Facilty Director	*Assoc. Teacher	Lead Teacher	Facilty Director	Assoc. Teacher	Lead Teacher	Facilty Director	Assoc. Teacher	Lead Teacher	Facilty Directo r
Teaching Staff • Registered for the 40-hour training within 90 days of hire • 40-hour certification completed within one year of hire • 5 Hour Literacy completed • Current & Valid Staff Credential issued by DCF for 20 to 39 children & a second for each additl. 20 children	40-Hour Certification + 5 Hour Literacy or Approved Equivalent	√	√	√	√	√	√	√	√	√	√	√	√
	HS Diploma or GED	25%	√	√	50%	√	√	75%	√	√	√	√	√
	Current & Valid EC Staff Credential issued by DCF	25%	75%	√	*50%	90%	√	75%	√	√	√	√	√
	One 3 credit ECE class or 45 hours informal ECE training ***	25%	75%	√	50%	90%	√	75%	90%	√	75%	√	√
Facility Director	12 ECE Cr. Hrs								25%	√	25%	√	√
• Level I or II Director credential	Advanced Dir. Credential									√			√
	• Associate degree with 12 ECE credits or • 60 credits with 12 ECE credits or • Bachelor degree or higher with 12 ECE credits								**25%	**√		**50%	**√
10 Hr State In-service Requirement	Annual 50 Points	25 % Professional Staff			50 % Professional Staff			75 % Professional Staff			100 % Professional Staff		

At the 2 and 3 star level, associate teachers without staff qualifications, hired six months prior to assessment may or may not be counted in Professional Development assessment, to be assessed to the advantage of the PD star rating. This decision will be made by the Program Owner/Director prior to assessment. If a program chooses to not have an associate teacher as part of the Professional Development assessment the associate teacher category can only achieve up to a 3 star to then be averaged with the other professional staff positions.

By October 1, 2012 the 4-Star and 5-Star levels will require an Associate Degree or higher with 12 ECE credits or 60

credits with 12 ECE credits for the percentage (%) of Lead Teachers and Directors as indicated in Staff Qualifications.

One formal 3 credit ECE class or 45 hours informal ECE training, to be met annually for each assessment cycle for staff that do not meet the 12 ECE credit hours or higher.

**** The 12 ECE Credit Benchmark can be met with related credits as determined and verified by the Registry.

A. EDUCATION POINTS ACHIEVED	B. POINTS REQUIRED	C. EXPERIENCE REDUCES TOTAL REQUIRED POINTS
		• 5 points for three years of documented full time service in current setting • 5 points maximum per assessment period for approved professional contributions experience • 5 points will be awarded to the Director for completing the Trainer Approval Series

Appendix 5E

PALM BEACH QIS FORM ON STAFF: CHILD RATIO AND GROUP SIZE

CENTER:

REVIEWER:

DATE:

NAME OF ROOM	LEAD TEACHER	NAMES OF ADDITIONAL STAFF PRESENT	# OF STAFF PRESENT	# OF CHILDREN PRESENT	MAX. GROUP SIZE/# ALLOWED BY DIRECTOR

SIGNATURE________________________ DATE__________

(Director or Person in Charge)

Print Name________________________

Appendix 5F

Monthly Staff Turnover Report

	Month: ____________	Year: ____________	
Site Name:	Site Address:		
Director's Name:	Site Type: Center	FCCH	School Site

Please check the appropriate box and complete the requested information:

☐ This Site has <u>no Practitioner turnover</u> to report this month. (No one left and/or no one is new at the site)

☐ Practitioner(s) <u>no longer employed</u> at this Site during this month:

PRACTITIONER*			
Name	Position Title	Employment Start Date	Employment End Date
1.			
2.			
3.			

*To report additional former employees, please use back of form.

☐ Practitioner(s) <u>new</u> at this Site during this month:

PRACTITIONER** Newly employed Practitioners must complete and return a Registry Practitioner Application.		
Name	Position Title	Employment Start Date
1.		
2.		
3.		

**To report additional new employees, please use back of form.

Director Signature________________________________ Date____________

Please complete and return completed form by the 30th of each month

Section III. Evaluation of the Quality Rating and Improvement System in Palm Beach County

6

Participation in and Reflection on Palm Beach County's Quality Improvement System: Perspectives from Practitioners

XINGYUAN GAO, JIANGANG XIA, JIANPING SHEN, AND XIN MA

Introduction

In this chapter, we first introduce the five clusters of interventions embedded in Palm Beach County's Quality Improvement System (QIS). Then we use these five clusters as a framework to evaluate, based on qualitative and quantitative data collected from 144 practitioners, their participation in and reflection on Palm Beach County's QIS. With this chapter, we transit into the evaluation of Palm Beach County's QIS from various perspectives.

Five Clusters of QIS

Palm Beach County's QIS was established with a focus on five clusters of interventions, including (a) education and training; (b) technical assistance; (c) support; (d) assessment, and (e) outreach. For the logic model, please refer to chapter 3.

Education and Training Cluster.

The education and training cluster is part of QIS that designed to help practitioners make progress in professional development. Buysse, Winton, and Rous (2009) defined "professional development" in early care and education as a term that "encompasses all types of facilitated learning opportunities" (p. 238). Through taking university courses, attending conferences and workshops, practitioners whose sites have participated in Palm Beach County's QIS would receive various opportunities to develop their professionalism.

Technical Assistance Cluster.

This cluster consists of programs and activities that enhance practitioners and early childhood providers' performance and level of star-rating scores with the assistance from on-site coaches and career advisors. Intensive on-site coaching has been proved to be effective in bringing positive changes to early care and education (ECE) teachers (Joyce & Showers, 2003; Neuman & Cunningham, 2009). Neuman and Cunningham (2009) compared three groups of ECE teachers, one group with coursework support alone, one group with coursework plus coaching, and a control group in language and literacy practices. The result showed that the group which received coursework and coaching demonstrated higher quality practices. Joyce and Showers (2003) found that coached teachers have following positive changes:

- practice new strategies more often and with greater skill than uncoached educators with identical initial training.
- adapted the strategies more appropriately to their own goals and contexts than did uncoached teachers who tended to practice observed or demonstrated lessons.
- retained and increased their skill over time—uncoached teachers did not.
- were more likely to explain the new models of teaching to their students, ensuring that students understood the purpose of their strategy and the behaviors expected of them.
- demonstrated a clearer understanding of the purposes and use of the new strategies. The frequent peer discussions about them, including lessons and materials design, seemed to enable them to 'think' with the strategies in ways which uncoached teachers never showed. (pp. 3–4)

Support Cluster.

The support cluster is composed of financial incentives, the QIS database, and the training registry. Specifically, financial incentives such as scholarships, quality enhancement payments, wage supplements, and awards are widely used in different sites to support and motivate practitioners. In Florida, the Work and Gain Economic Self-Sufficiency (WAGE$) program is developed to "improve child care quality by reducing turnover and encouraging the continued education of early childhood teachers" (Florida Children's Forum, 2011, p. 19). At Miami-Dade County, researchers found educators who received WAGE$ remained in their jobs longer than those who did not participate in the program. Besides, 17% of WAGE$ participants upgraded their education degree on the WAGE$ salary supplement scale (Florida Children's Forum, 2011). In addition, another program, the Seek Excellence in Education and Knowledge (SEEK) scholarship program, allocates funds for practitioners to pursue formal and informal continuing education. The SEEK scholarship program is open to all members of the Registry of the Palm Beach State College (http://www.pbcregistry.org).

Assessment Cluster.

According to the standards of the six pathways to quality, Palm Beach County's QIS establishes the star rating system to assess, communicate, and improve the quality of participating early care and education sites. The six pathways to quality are: (a) Environment; (b) Professional Development; (c) Staff-to-Child Ratio and Group Size (applying to child care centers and school-based childcare sites only); (d) Administration and Business Management (applying to family childcare homes only); (e) Parent Involvement; (f) Program (curriculum); and (g) Child Developmental Screenings. Each of the pathways has achievable standards for assessments, the results of assessments then are used to compute as a star rating score. Among the six pathways to quality, Environment and Professional Development are regarded as the key pathways. Therefore, they received greater weight in star rating.

Outreach Cluster.

Public and consumers' awareness and access to quality care are also valued by the Palm Beach County's QIS. The outreach cluster is related to the activities such as marketing and networking. Through those activities, parents are kept informed of a QIS childcare site's quality. Schilder et al. (2011) claimed that QIS can improve communication among parents, providers, and policymakers at the quality level in early education and care and out of school time/after-school settings.

All five clusters described above are interconnected as a systematic approach to significantly enhancing the quality of early care and education sites in Palm Beach County. In this chapter, the five clusters were utilized as categories to classify and analyze the 144 practitioners' feedbacks with respect to strengths and suggestions for improvement.

Practitioner as Important Stakeholder

Many scholars have pointed out that practitioners are fundamental to the quality of early care and education (e.g., Buysse & Hollingsworth, 2009; Early & Winton, 2001; Saracho & Spodek, 2007). Phillips, Mekos, Scarr, McCartney, and Abbott-Shim (2000) compared education quality of childcare centers located in Boston, Virginia, and Atlanta. Their findings indicated that both education and training of teachers significantly predict the quality of classroom interactions for the infants and toddlers. Moreover, Vu, Jeon, and Howes (2008)'s study showed that among 231 classrooms sponsored by 122 different agencies, not only teachers' education and credential level are associated with classroom quality, but also the credential level of the program director can predict the classroom quality. Therefore, the extent of practitioners' participation in QIS, as well as their perspectives on the strengths and weaknesses of the QIS, calls for the attention of policy makers, program designers, and researchers.

A Brief Note on the Research Methods of the Chapter

The evaluation questions in this chapter include: (a) What are the extent of practitioners' participation in various QIS components? (b) From the view of early childcare practitioners, what are QIS's strengths and limitations? The questionnaire was sent via e-mail addresses obtained from Palm Beach Community College's database. Practitioners had sufficient time (two weeks) to finish the online questionnaire. Among 640 practitioners, 144 of them returned completed questionnaire. In the questionnaire, all practitioners were asked to report their level of participation in QIS and write down three major strengths and three major limitations of QIS. In the following, based on quantitative data, we tallied the reports of practitioners' participation in QIS and then analyzed the patterns of their involvement and satisfaction. Based on the qualitative data, we used the five clusters as the framework to code the data and developed themes of strengths and weaknesses for the five clusters, respectively. The process of theme generation is to find out the patterns evident in the setting and conveyed by the participants (Marshall & Rossman, 2011). Our decision rule for the theme is that at least 10% (around 15) of practitioners have mentioned the same strengths or weaknesses if a strength or weakness is to qualify as a theme.

Extent of Practitioners' Participation in QIS

Rates of participation in various QIS components

According to the QIS practitioner survey with 144 respondents, 76% of the respondents know QIS well. It appears that there is variation in the participation rate, ranging from 51% for college courses to 91% for career advisors. The utilization rates for various QIS interventions are shown in Table 6.1. The appendixes of the report contain detailed technical information for the data source, such as sample size, response rate, and data analysis approach. The main report will not repeat the technical information to reduce repetitiveness.

Table 6.1: *Utilization of QIS Interventions*

Interventions	% of respondents who utilized QIS Intervention
Workshops and conferences approved by the Registry	79
College courses	51
Early learning coach	83
Career advisor	91
WAGE$	53
SEEK scholarship	83

Consistency in Participation in Various QIS Components

As part of the practitioner survey, one correlation analysis was performed to examine the issue of consistency of participation by QIS practitioners in various programs (the WAGE$ program, early learning coaches, career advisors, workshops and conferences, and college course credits). Table 6.2 shows that QIS practitioners who utilize the WAGE$ program also work more frequently with career advisors. QIS practitioners who spend more hours working with early learning coaches also (a) attend more workshops and conferences approved by the Registry, (b) earn more college course credits, and in particular (c) work more often with career advisors. Finally, QIS practitioners who work more often with career advisors also attend more workshops and conferences approved by the Registry.

Table 6.2: *Consistency of Participation in Various Programs*

	1	2	3	4	5
1. Utilizing WAGE$ program	1.000				
2. Number of hours working with early learning coaches	.096	1.000			
3. Number of times working with career advisors	.243*	.405*	1.000		
4. Number of attended workshops and conferences approved by the Registry	.091	.315*	.359*	1.000	
5. Number of college course credits earned with the support of QIS	.099	.342*	.166	.194	1.000

Note. * $p < .05$. Consistency is measured through correlation coefficient.

Among these statistically significant correlations, the largest correlation (0.405) is between the number of hours working with early learning coaches and the number of times working with career advisors, whereas the smallest correlation (0.243) is between utilizing the WAGE$ program and the number of times working with career advisors. Therefore, QIS practitioners who work more actively with early learning coaches also work more actively with career advisors.

Practitioners' Perceived Effectiveness of Various QIS Components

Effectiveness of Various QIS Components

According to the QIS practitioner survey, it appears that overall participants felt the interventions are effective, with percentages of perceived effectiveness ranging from 61% for WAGE$ to 92% for SEEK scholarship. Table 6.3 shows the percentage of perceived effectiveness for components of the QIS intervention.

Table 6.3 : *Percentage of Those Who Were Exposed to QIS Interventions and Felt the Intervention Effective*

Interventions	Percentage
WAGE$	61
Early learning coach	80
Career advisor	69
SEEK scholarship	92
Workshops and conferences approved by the Registry	89
College courses	72

Consistency in the Impact of Various QIS Components

The data from this section come from the practitioners' survey. One correlation analysis is performed to examine the issue of consistency in terms of effects of various programs (the WAGE$ program, early learning coaches, career advisors, workshops and conferences, and college course credits) on improvement of job skills, impact on respondents' career, and the decision to stay at their current facility. Table 6.4 shows that QIS practitioners who decide to stay at their current facility because of the WAGE$ program also experience a larger impact on their career as a result of working with career advisors. In other words, QIS practitioners who benefit more from the WAGE$ program also benefit more from career advisors. Improvement of job skills as a result of working with early learning coaches is not related to improvement of job skills as a result of any other program, indicating the unique independency of the early learning coaches program.

Table 6.4: *Consistency of Effects of Various Programs*

	1	2	3	4	5
1. WAGE$ program	1.000				
2. Early learning coaches	.206	1.000			
3. Career advisors	.317*	.056	1.000		
4. SEEK scholarship	.107	.162	.563*	1.000	
5. Workshops and conferences approved by the Registry	.201	.184	.356*	.467*	1.000

Note. * $p < .05$. Consistency is measured through correlation coefficient.

QIS practitioners who experience greater improvement of job skills as a result of working with career advisors also experience greater improvement of job skills as a result of (a) utilizing SEEK scholarship and (b) attending workshops and conferences approved by the Registry. Stated differently, QIS practitioners who benefit more from career advisors also benefit more from (a) SEEK scholarship and (b) workshops and conferences approved by the Registry.

Finally, QIS practitioners who experience greater improvement of job skills as a result of utilizing SEEK scholarship also experience greater improvement of job skills as a result of attending workshops and conferences approved by the Registry. In other words, QIS practitioners who benefit more from SEEK scholarship also benefit more from workshops and conferences approved by the Registry.

Among these statistically significant correlations, the largest correlation (0.563) corresponds to program effects between career advisors and SEEK scholarship, whereas the smallest correlation (0.317) corresponds to program effects between the WAGE$ program and career advisors. Therefore, the largest consistency of program effects is between working with career advisors and utilizing SEEK scholarship. In other words, the most evident phenomenon associated with QIS is that QIS practitioners who experience a larger impact on their careers as a result of working with career advisors also experience greater improvement of job skills as a result of utilizing SEEK scholarship.

Overall Strengths and Weaknesses of the QIS Perceived by Practitioners

Practitioners identified strengths and limitations of QIS in the practitioner survey. With the 10% cut-off point, we coded the strengths and limitations under five clusters: (a) education and training, (b) technical assistance, (c) support, (d) assessment, and (e) outreach. Given the 10% cut-off point, no themes occurred in the "outreach" cluster since few practitioners talked about it.

Education and Training

To develop professionalism among early care and education practitioners whose site joined QIS, various university courses, conference and workshops are available to practitioners. The results of our survey indicate that practitioners regard opportunities to get educated and trained as a strength of QIS. In the meantime, they believe they have made progress in those programs or activities, and their attitudes toward professionalism are greatly enhanced. However, practitioners feel that there is a need for some improvements in the amount and content of education and training.

Strength of the Education and Training Cluster.

The strength related to the education and training cluster mentioned most frequently by practitioners is the variety of choices for education and training, including college courses for degrees and certification as well as workshops and conferences. Sixteen practitioners reported QIS had its strength in providing "a wide range" of training courses, conferences, and workshops to teachers. Most practitioners appreciated the "opportunities for learning through workshops and conferences" or that "provide teachers the opportunity to receive a better education." Among all the education and training activities, workshop was most frequently mentioned by practitioners.

The second theme of strength that emerged is that many practitioners felt that they had made progress in knowledge and skills through education and training provided by QIS. One practitioner wrote that "professional development training requirements enhance and sharpen necessary skills." Another practitioner reported "increase(d) knowledge about child growth and development." Among those practitioners who mentioned workshops, one found "tools learned in workshops" made him or her "work(s) better with our clients."

The third theme of the education and training cluster suggests that more than 10% of practitioners felt motivated as a result of their involvement in education and training activities. They were encouraged by the progress they had made toward professionalism through QIS education and training. One practitioner succinctly wrote "encourage professionalism." One commented that "trained associates are more confident, and parents are confident when associates are trained professionals." Notably, one respondent observed that practitioners were "better trained and they stay at the center longer due to being able to get their classes and workshops paid for," which may imply a virtuous circle in that practitioners were increasingly devoted to their profession when receiving even more professional development training and education.

Limitation of the Education and Training Cluster.

The first limitation of this cluster is that the amount of training provided by QIS still did not meet the need of practitioners. Seventeen practitioners wished there were more training or workshops available to them in terms of the format, location, or time. In other words, QIS needs to provide more flexibility to practitioners. Practitioners thought that they need more "online workshops" or "internet classes," "workshops in our area" or "at the school site," "workshops during working hours" or "on practitioner workdays," "equal amount of training time for each age group," and "better time frame for meeting other than night."

The content of education and training is the second issue emerged from this cluster; at least 15 teachers were concerned about how to make the professional training more aligned with practitioners' practice. One practitioner suggested that "professional development needs to be reviewed" or "revised" so that it could "be more realistic," another expressed similar ideas by stating that "QIS needs to be more specific in what they really desire in a well-rounded curriculum." Other practitioners suggested more workshops and conferences "that teach QIS methods in various topics," "on practitioner skills for QIS," "on the tool systems," and "on classroom management and challenging behavior."

Technical Assistance

Coaching is considered most helpful by practitioners; nevertheless, practitioners suggested that it would be even better if QIS could have more coaches who were well trained. Although the career advisor is one of the major components in the technical assistance cluster, we found less than 10% of practitioners have mentioned them; therefore, we do not have themes related to career advisors.

Strength of the Technical Assistance Cluster.

As far as the QIS technical assistance is concerned, 38 practitioners highly recommended its on-site coaching assistance. Practitioners referred "coach" to either coach as a person to assist or coaching as the activities, or both. For example, one practitioner wrote "dedication from the coach (patience)," another practitioner mentioned "they help you learn new ways to help the children learn," and still another wrote that "coaching? the support is wonderful. Our center has benefited greatly and learned so much from each coach assigned to our center."

Although most practitioners only wrote "coach" and did not give specific reasons why they thought "coach" was a strength of the technical assistance cluster, we did find comments providing some description about how coaches could help them improve and in what areas they need help. For instance, one practitioner spoke highly of the coaches for "helping us to ensure that licensing and accreditation standards are met and exceeded," other practitioners appreciated "coach" for "pointing out your weaknesses" or "they help you learn new ways to help the children learn." Among all comments, there is a very detailed comment by a practitioner who offered a very clear picture about which areas coaches helped make improvement, how they assisted practitioners, and coached them through various activities: "The early learning coach gives lots of support, guidance and knowledge with classroom arrangements, lesson plan improvements, demonstrating small and large group activities with the children, great techniques for classroom management, transitional times and cool down activities."

Another characteristic of coaching that is favored by practitioners is its accessibility. Among practitioners who mentioned "coach/coaching" as strength, 7 practitioners considered that coaches were easy to access when they need help. One practitioner wrote the following: "if you need the answers, they are there to help."

Limitation of the Technical Assistance Cluster.

The limitation of the technical assistance cluster is also about coach or coaching, the suggestions on coaching primarily refer to teachers' need of more coaching. Among the 20 respondents who made suggestions, 9 of them requested either "more time" working with the quality coach, or expected that the coach could make "more visits" to the centers or the coach could "spend more time in the centers." One teacher suggested that the coaches "need to come to centers more than once a week." Another group of teachers refer to an individual coach's professional attitude. One teacher suggested that the coach should be "open minded" because the teacher felt that the coach "wanted everything her way or no way," while another teacher noticed that "coach not up to date with reports before the visits to the centers." Teachers were also concerned about coach's experience. One teacher noticed that some coaches "have not had experience teaching or doing the things they are telling staff to do."

Support

As we have introduced in the foregoing, WAGE$ and SEEK are the two primary financial incentives for early childcare practitioners to participate in QIS program. The responses from the 144 practitioners confirmed the strengths of the two programs and provided suggestions for improvement as well.

Strengths of the Support Cluster.

In terms of its strengths, 35 practitioners mentioned SEEK scholarship, and 19 practitioners referred to WAGE$. Among those 35 teachers who wrote about scholarship, 19 teachers specifically mentioned "SEEK" scholarship, while the other 16 teachers talked about financial incentives for their education in general terms. As teachers "wouldn't be able to afford taking college classes on their salaries," SEEK Scholarship is welcomed by teachers for its "wonderful resource for all of our teachers." Respondents mentioned how SEEK made their pursuit of academic degree possible, teachers said "through SEEK scholarship we are able to prepare a pay for classes," "I can go back to school and finish getting my degree," and "QIS has given us the opportunity to go back to school by providing the SEEK scholarship."Especially, one teacher explained how the scholarship program could not only benefit one in the short-term but also benefit everyone in the long-run by promoting a better learning environment for all practitioners: "my current education is all towards my 4yr degree in teaching with QIS now in our school the others around me are being educated to understand why I act a certain way around the children. Thus staff member are more aware of their actions around the children!"

The WAGE$ program was also highly welcomed by many QIS practitioners. Among the 19 practitioners who mentioned WAGE$ as a strength, 10 teachers specifically referred to "WAGE$" program, while the other 9 practitioners mentioned incentives in general terms. They felt that "a little bit of extra money is always good," "wages is great for the teachers to supplement their income." The practitioners' responses showed that how they felt being inspired by higher wages. One teacher commented that "the school is able to receive funding and help the staff feel more appreciated and want to continue working for better results." Other teachers said the WAGE$ program "gives an incentive to be better teachers" and is "very helpful in retaining employees."

Limitations of the Support Cluster.

Among the 144 responses, 19 practitioners mentioned that the QIS had limitations in its support aspects. Almost all the 19 practitioners expressed their desire to have better pay or more incentive such as SEEK scholarship and WAGE$. However, the specific suggestions for the SEEK scholarship program and the WAGE$ program were diverse. For example, several practitioners had suggestions for the SEEK scholarship; they hoped that the SEEK scholarship could either be increased, or extended to cover online courses, or extended to pay for master's degrees. Some practitioners—they might be directors of the childcare sites—suggested a WAGE$ program for directors as well. For instance, one practitioner suggested that "director should be able to receive wages," while another practitioner proposed that "we spend time in every classroom and should be awarded for that."

Assessment

Among Palm Beach County's six QIS components, three activities were related to assessment: (a) the achievable standards, (b) the star ratings, and (c) the reliable assessments. Further, the Children's Services Council of Palm Beach County used, among others, two instruments to collect data as quality indicators of centers: the Early Childhood Environmental Rating Scale (ECERS) evaluates child care centers serving children from age 2.5 to 5, and the Infant/Toddler Environmental Scale (ITERS) evaluates childcare centers serving children from birth to age 2.5. In total, 43 items in ECERS and 39 items in ITERS are organized into six common scales: space and furnishing, personal care routines, language reasoning, activities, interactions, and program structure. The 144 practitioners participated in the survey paid much attention to the strengths and limitations of QIS assessment with respect to the standards, ratings, and the specific scales such as space and furnishing.

Strengths of the Assessment Cluster.

Among the 144 practitioners, 18 practitioners mentioned "standards" as a strength of QIS, while 25 practitioners mentioned specifically "the guidance for the classroom set up" as a strength of QIS. Practitioners confirmed that QIS standards were essential for enhancing childcare quality. For instance, one practitioner wrote that "by raising the standards of required guidelines, rules and regulations in every area," the QIS "enhances the quality of the school for children, staff and parents"; another practitioner believed that "high standards" helped "to uphold quality childcare." More practitioners referred to the specific guidelines (common scales) that QIS aimed to evaluate; 25 practitioners mentioned about classroom set up or classroom arrangement. Practitioners liked that QIS "showing us different ways to set up our rooms," "helps teachers to enhance early learning environments," and thus created "enough room for the children to play safely."

Limitations of the Assessment Cluster.

Among the 144 responses, 46 practitioners mentioned the suggestions for improving QIS on its assessment aspect (42 practitioners) and standards aspect (22 practitioners). Some other themes will not be discussed in this chapter because of the 10% cut-off point that we set for the analyses in this chapter. The assessment issues that practitioners complained primarily include three aspects: assessor, scheduling, and scoring. The assessor issues mainly referred to the consistency of assessment process. One practitioner complained that the assessor had "too many personal opinions," another practitioner wrote that "assessors need to follow the scale not their personal opinions." Thus, sometimes the assessments were perceived to be "subjective to the individual assessor's perspective and experiences" and "the assessments are not consistent; it differs depending on the reviewer."One example was that "in one year something in the environment is o.k. and scores high. The next year the same thing in the environment is not o.k. and scores low. Sometimes from one classroom to the next there are inconsistencies. Also consistency from one assessor to the next assessor can differ." As a result, some practitioners suggested that we need to "get the same assessor or same two assessors for the entire assessment so things are fairer," or "we prefer same assessor for entire school", while other practitioners suggested "better training for the assessor."

Under the assessment cluster, the scheduling issue was another concern. First, teachers felt that the one-month time frame was too long, and thus one teacher suggested that "visits and assessments to centers should be in a smaller time frame (shorter than three weeks)," while another teacher advocated that "instead of one whole month waiting for the assessors, could the time soon be two weeks?" Second, for the length and frequency of assessment, teachers had different ideas. One teacher was concerned about the length of evaluation and expected that they could have "more than 1 day for evaluation." Other teachers suggested various assessment frequencies ranging from "every other year" to "twice during the year", and "three times a year." One teacher complained that they "do not have an assessment in the summer." Third, teachers also made several suggestions concerning more detailed announcements with day and time of the monitoring, flexible deadlines, and avoiding being around holidays. Some suggestions do have practical impact on the assessment. For instance, one teacher believed that it would be good if assessments were "not around holidays, right after/before a long vacation (actual school breaks not personal), so that children are able to get back into routine."

Besides the assessor and scheduling aspects, several teachers mentioned QIS scoring issues, and almost all the suggestions about scoring referred to the practice that QIS used the lowest score across all classes that monitored. As an alternative, teachers suggested to "combine all scores from all the classrooms into one score" or use the average so that the assessment can "come to a fair conclusion." One teacher suggested that "Parent assessments of the center should be required and impact our score." Another teacher also mentioned that the "Clarifications on Scoring" needs to be improved.

The issue of standards was mainly directed to the standards used for assessment and the health and safety requirements. The first group of suggestions was about the QIS standards and its coordination with some other program standards such as High Scope and Head Start. One practitioner complained that "It feels at times that the standards come from people that do not work with children on an everyday basis and do not realize how some of these regulations are difficult to understand," while another practitioner noticed that "standards & expectations within pathways seem to increase with each year." As a result, some practitioners felt that the "expectations are too high" and "some areas are beyond our control as teachers." One practitioner appealed that "stop being so hard on staff when we are used to doing things according to the head start standards." Another practitioner suggested that "I feel that QIS should work together with other childcare agencies such as High Scope and the health department so that their requirements wouldn't conflict as much as they do."

The second group of suggestions was about QIS health and safety requirements. The specific QIS hand-washing requirement was mentioned six times by practitioners. They complained that kids were "washing hands all the time," and the hand washing requirements/procedures are "obsessive," "too lengthy," and even "crazy." One practitioner challenged the hand washing requirement by saying that "I do not feel washing hands after a child touches EVERY single thing is practical. Germs are everywhere, and washing their hands after eating and before eating, after the bathroom and after certain things are more practical than after every little thing." On the QIS safety requirements, practitioners also had much to say. One practitioner complained that "safety procedure is out of a teacher's hands." "I am very aware and keep my children in a safe environment at all times," the practitioner continued, "but no matter what you do it is never good enough." One practitioner suggested that "environment safety should be based on local and state regulations not necessarily that of a national requirement."

Concluding Remarks

Participation Rates and Level of Perceived Effectiveness

Our survey indicates that most QIS practitioners were familiar with QIS and that they participated in one or more components of QIS. The correlation analysis revealed the pattern that practitioners who utilized some components of QIS were likely to use some other components. A further examination revealed that the impacts of each component of QIS were not only effective but also correlated. Our findings showed one or more components among WAGE$ program, early learning coaches, career advisors, workshops and conferences, and college course credits had an influence on improvement of job skills, an impact on respondents' career, and the decision to stay at their current facility. Therefore, the practitioners were generally satisfied with QIS. Moreover, the consistency in participation in various QIS components and the consistency among the effects of different QIS programs implied that the interconnections of QIS components were strong and reliable in practice as the system designers expected. For more findings on the impact of QIS in practitioners, center quality, and center-level school readiness, please see other chapters in the book.

Strengths and Suggestions

Just like what was revealed by the quantitative data, qualitative data also revealed that practitioners were satisfied with QIS; the suggestions were related to the details of implementation rather than the overall design of QIS.

According to the qualitative comments from practitioners, QIS had three strengths in the education and training cluster. First, QIS provided a variety of opportunities, including college courses, workshops and conferences. Second, education and training programs offered by QIS were effective in improving practitioners' knowledge and skills. Third, practitioners reported being motivated through learning to be more professional. However, practitioners also suggested that there should be more content and delivery methods.

As far as the technical assistance cluster was concerned, coaching was considered most useful to practitioners in updating practical knowledge about communicating with children, classroom management, and transitional time. Accessibility was another strength of coaching; practitioners suggested that they could always find their coaches when they needed advice or help. Practitioners suggested more coaching would be beneficial to them.

In terms of financial support, both SEEK and WAGE$ were welcomed for practitioners and childcare sites. Practitioners suggested that the supports can either be increased or extended to cover more education opportunities.

As for assessment, the first strength generally referred to the belief that QIS standards helped enhancing the quality of childcare. The second strength lay in the specific QIS guideline for classroom arrangement. Practitioners also mentioned some suggestions for (a) assessment which were centered around assessors, scheduling, and scoring, and for (b) standards which were mostly directed to the standards used for assessment and the health and safety requirements.

The Absence of the Outreach Cluster in Practitioners' Responses

Given the 10% cut-off point to quality for a theme, we did not find any themes related to the outreach cluster. We noticed practitioners commented on those QIS components that were related more closely to their professional life—they had more feedback on the first four clusters, but not the fifth cluster of "outreach." It is understandable that almost all practitioners directly took part in the various activities from the first four clusters, but fewer practitioners engaged in "outreaching" activities such as marketing or networking. In fact, "outreaching" was more in the QIS system than at the individual practitioner's level. However, the findings also pointed out that the work related to the outreaching cluster should be emphasized more.

References

Buysse, V., & Hollingsworth, H. L. (2009). Program quality and early childhood inclusion: Recommendations for professional development. *Topics in Early Childhood Special Education*, 29(2), 119–128.

Buysse, V., Winton, P. J., & Rous, B. (2009). Reaching consensus on a definition of professional development for the early childhood field. *Topics in Early Childhood Special Education, 28*(4), 235–243.

Early, D. M., & Winton, P. J. (2001). Preparing the workforce: Early childhood teacher preparation at 2-and 4-year institutions of higher education. *Early Childhood Research Quarterly, 16*, 285–306.

Florida Children's Forum. (2011). *Miami-Dade County Quality Counts workforce study.* Tallahassee, FL: Florida Children's Forum. Retrieved February 2012 from http://www.fcforum.org/downloads/publications/QCCC%20Workforce%20Study.pdf.

Joyce, B., & Showers, B. (2003). *Student achievement through staff development.* Retrieved February 2012 from http://literacy.kent.edu/coaching/information/Research/randd-engaged-joyce.pdf.

Marshall, C., & Rossman, G. B. (2011). *Designing qualitative research.* (5th ed). Thousand Oaks, CA: Sage Publications.

Neuman, S. B., & Cunningham, L. (2009). The impact of professional development and coaching on early language and literacy instructional practices. *American Educational Research Journal, 46*, 532–566.

Phillips, D. A., Mekos, D., Scarr, S., McCartney, K., & Abbott-Shim, M. (2000).Within and beyond the classroom door: Assessing quality in child care centers. *Early Childhood Research Quarterly, 15*, 475–496.

Saracho, O. N., & Spodek, B. (2007). Early childhood teachers' preparation and the quality of program outcomes. *Early Childhood Development and Care, 177*(1), 71–91.

Schilder, D., Young, J., Anastasopoulos, L., Kimura, S., & Rivera, B. (2011). *Massachusetts quality rating and improvement system provisional standards study: Final report.* Boston, MA: Massachusetts Department of Early Education and Care.

Vu, J., Jeon, H.-J., & Howes, C. (2008). Formal education, credential, or both: Early childhood program classroom practices. *Early Education and Development, 19*, 479–504.

7

Effects of Quality Improvement System on Early Childhood Education Practitioners

JIANPING SHEN, XIN MA, WENDY TACKETT, XUEJIN LU, KAREN BRANDI, JEFF GOODMAN, LANCE TILL, AND GRACE WATSON

Introduction

Friendly, Doherty, and Beach (2006) attributed the lack of national standards for early childhood education to "different perceptions of childhood and the purpose of ELCC (early learning and child care)" (p. 15). Guided by a general research consensus in the early childhood education literature that "specific conditions are essential at the system level to ensure that high quality at the program level is the norm rather than the exception" (Friendly et al., 2006, p. 15), many state childcare agencies have chosen to set general goals to create healthy childcare environments, provide training and formal education for providers of programs, strengthen professional development systems, and promote emotionally supportive caregiving (Pittard, Zaslow, Lavelle, & Porter, 2006).

The Quality Improvement System (QIS) designed and implemented in Palm Beach County, Florida, is such a system-level initiative. It is a comprehensive, voluntary, early care and education improvement system that aims to improve the quality of childcare from birth to age 5. QIS seeks to prepare children to be eager and ready to learn when it is time for them to enter schooling. QIS started with a group of local early childhood education advocates who worked together for over a year to design a comprehensive, customized early care and education quality improvement system for licensed childcare sites, school-based childcare sites, and family childcare homes who hold a rate agreement with the county government to accept children receiving subsidies. Apart from these individual childcare sites, multiple collaborative agencies were involved with QIS, including the Children's Services Council of Palm Beach County; Early Learning Coalition of Palm Beach County; Palm Beach Community College; School District of Palm Beach County; Family Central, Inc.; Palm Beach County Health Department; Health Care District of Palm Beach County; Palm Beach County Child Care Directors Association; and Palm Beach County Family Child Care Association.

The initial ideas of QIS were then put into a local pilot program, the Picower Quality Child Care Initiative. Based on results from this pilot, Palm Beach County finalized the goals of QIS in 2003 as (a) producing positive outcomes for children; (b) providing consumer education to help parents recognize, expect and seek out quality in a child care setting; and (c) defining, advocating for, and obtaining the resources necessary to encourage, support, and promote quality early care and education.

Specifically, QIS contains six components. The first component, six pathways to quality, emphasizes environment, professional development, staff-to-child ratio (i.e., group size) (for childcare centers and school-based childcare sites), administration and business management (for family childcare homes), parental involvement, program (curriculum), and child developmental screenings. The second component, achievable standards, provides a fair system for assessing and rating a childcare site and develops a roadmap for achieving high quality. The third component, star ratings, indicates to what extent a childcare site has met general quality criteria. The fourth component, reliable assessments, ensures a fair, consistent, and accurate assessment process for each participating childcare site by adopting nationally recognized, research-based program assessment tools to assess the quality of the childcare sites. The fifth component, quality improvement supports, provides financial and technical supports to childcare sites and their staff to participate in QIS. The final component, consumer education opportunities, informs current and future parents and staff of a childcare site's commitment to enhanced quality through its participation in QIS.

QIS delivered a range of programs to help early childhood education practitioners to improve their job skills and knowledge base. Both early learning coaches program and career advisors program paired practitioners with coaches to form training mentorship and advisors to provide career guidance. The Palm Beach County Registry approved and offered workshops and conferences for practitioners to attend to earn credits for certificate and degree purposes. As incentives for participating in training and technical assistance programs, two different incentives were also offered. The SEEK scholarship program allocated funds for practitioners to pursue continuing education. The WAGE$ program aims to retain early childhood educators by providing education-based wage supplements to low-paid practitioners working with children 0–5 years of age. When this study was conducted, "low-paid" was defined as "less than $17.50 per hour," and the annual supplement ranged from $200 for a Childhood Development Associate (CDA) or the equivalent of $3,000 for those with a bachelor's degree in early childhood education or its equivalent. These QIS programs have been implemented for five years. This research was motivated by the following research question: Did these QIS programs significantly improve the job skills and knowledge base of early childhood education practitioners?

In line with Katz (1993), we argue that there are four ways to assess change in the quality of early childhood education programs as a result of educational intervention: (a) identify characteristics of the setting, equipment, and program that have been altered; (b) determine any change as experienced by the children served; (c) assess any change as experienced by the families served; and (d) consider any change as experienced by the responsible staff. We took the last strategy in this research to examine the effects of QIS on early childhood education practitioners. Although we studied the perceptions of practitioners, the findings were corroborated by another study we conducted that focused on pre- and post-observations using the Early Childhood Environmental Rating Scale (ECERS), the Infant/Toddler Environmental Scale (ITERS), and their revised versions of ECERS-R and ITERS-R (Ma et al., 2011).

Review of Research Literature

The Importance of Quality Early Childhood Education

It has been known that high-quality early childhood experiences are a major factor in children's development and their ability to succeed once they reach school and beyond. Recent evidence from the field of neuroscience once again highlights the vital importance of early childhood education—the quality of children's early education experiences directly affects their sense of security, brain development, and subsequent ability to learn and reason; in particular, critical connective pathways need to be established in the brain during the early years of child development to avoid potential learning difficulties later in life (Committee on Integrating the

Science of Early Childhood Development, 2000). The classic assertion of Barnett (1995) and Entwisle (1995) stated that high quality preschool experiences boost academic achievement and social adjustment later in school, reduce the likelihood of retention or placement in special education, and increase the chance of graduation from high school (see also Greene, 2006). Among those cognitive factors that benefit from early childhood education, language stands out. According to Ludwig and Sawhill (2007), children who are exposed early to sophisticated vocabulary in conversations tend to be much better prepared for reading comprehension (see also National Research Council, 1999).

Early childhood education helps offset inequalities among children. The negative effects of poverty can be compensated by participation in high quality early childhood education programs (Schweinhart, Barnes, & Weikart, 1993). A number of randomized, controlled experiments showed that the lasting cognitive gains for children with high quality early childhood education are particularly large for the most disadvantaged children (e.g., Currie, 2000; Ramey & Ramey, 1998). Furthermore, the lasting cognitive gains are the largest for children whose mothers have the lowest levels of education (e.g., Waldfogel, 2002). Early childhood education is particularly important also to young English language learners for academic excellence in school and prevention of dropping out of school (Espinosa, 2008). Overall, early childhood education provides a solid foundation for P-16 (preschool to college) education promoting educational excellence, lifelong learning, and competitiveness in the job market (Takanishi & Kauerz, 2008).

Investment in quality early childhood education saves special education costs, social welfare, and correction costs. Based on findings from the High/Scope Perry Preschool project, Nelson (2006) stated that:

> Conservative cost-benefit models show that for an initial investment of roughly \$15,000 per child, the return to society was roughly \$250,000, or \$17 for every dollar invested. This return comprised savings in the areas of criminal justice system costs, education spending, and welfare costs. It also included increased tax revenue due to higher lifetime earnings of the cohort members. (p. 1)

Belfield (2004) estimated that P-K (preschool and kindergarten) education benefits offset from 41% to 62% of total spending on early childhood education in New York State. Therefore, to a large extent, early childhood education benefits both children and society (Lynch, 2004).

The Role of Skilled Practitioners in Improving the Quality of Early Childhood Education

What improves the quality of early childhood education? Based on findings from the High/Scope Perry Preschool project, Nelson (2006) described the features of a successful early childhood education program:

> [It] must include teachers with a bachelor's degree and certification in early childhood education; small class sizes (5–6 children); a minimum of two and one-half hours of instruction daily; weekly home visits; health and nutrition screening for children, and training for parents; and use of an instructional model that incorporates self-initiated, small- and large-group activities according to accepted, researched models of child development. (p. 1).

Among these features, some are highly emphasized in the early childhood education literature, two of which, as we noticed, are job skills and knowledge base. Generally supported by research, the National Association for the Education of Young Children (NAEYC) advocated a constellation of child-centered job skills or care practices for early childhood education practitioners as (a) serving as resources to children's self-initiated activities, (b) providing open-ended opportunities for children to explore concrete materials, (c) promoting interaction among children, (d) avoiding teaching basic skills using drill (practice) and workbooks (worksheets), and (e) embedding basic skills in meaningful everyday activities (see Bredekamp & Copple, 1997; Hart, Burts, & Charlesworth, 1997; Stipek & Byler, 1997).

The Role of Professional Development in Improving the Quality of Early Childhood Educators

Review of literature has pointed to evidence that professional development, both formal education and informal training, have produced positive impact on early childhood educators which can, in turn, lead to quality child care programs and significant improvement in child development (Landry et al., 2009). One of the important indicators that can lead to improved child outcomes is effective teacher-child interaction. Hamre, Pianta and Downer's (2009) study, with randomized control trial design, came to the conclusion that teachers who received course training in beliefs and knowledge related to the types of child-teacher interaction were more effective in daily interaction with children than those who were not involved in the course training. Their research findings have triangulated previous findings that quality teacher training and professional development can help build more effective teacher-child interactions and contribute positively to the child outcomes (NICHD ECCRN, 2002; Maxwell & Clifford, 2006; Pianta et al., 2008). Some other studies, with focus on the impact of professional development on childcare practitioners in general and on their self-improvement in particular, indicated that professional development activities lead to an increase in participants' sense of self-efficacy, including expressions of confidence in their own abilities in mathematics and reading (Ciyer et al., 2010) and improvement in language and literacy practices (Neuman & Cunningham, 2009), and eventually transfer their self-improvement into an overall higher quality care for children (Tout, Zaslow & Berry, 2006).

In the QIS context, professional development assisting childcare practitioners to obtain college degrees or certifications, as well as improving staff and directors' credentials are reported (e.g., Children's Forum, 2011; Shen et al., 2009). The importance of degrees and staff credentials is supported by the study conducted by University of Pittsburgh Office of Child Development (2006) regarding Pennsylvania's Keystone STARS Quality Rating System in childcare settings, which found that teachers with college degrees provide high quality early education and care. The recent literature review on the coaching practice in the field of early care and education programs by Child Trends (Isner et al., 2011) presents evidence that coaching, an individualized professional development strategy provided to the practitioners in QIS, holds promise for bringing about changes in practice and improving child outcomes. Research studies focusing on the impact of professional development on practitioners in the context of QIS are still limited, and this study contributes to the knowledge base.

Specialized early childhood education training affects early childhood education practitioners' behavior and the quality of their programs (Saracho & Spodek, 2007). According to these researchers, practitioners with a bachelor's degree are more responsive to children and provide more activities that promote language development and emergent literacy. Effective curriculum tied to high standards and strong instructional content are crucial in early childhood education programs (Kagan & Kauerz, 2006). The understanding and implementation of such an effective curriculum obviously require a strong knowledge base on early childhood education.

In agreement, we consider job skills and knowledge base as the key factors contributing to the quality of early childhood education. In this sense, the program efforts of QIS in improving job skills and knowledge base were expected to create positive changes among early childhood education practitioners. We evaluated the effects of various programs of QIS in an attempt to determine whether they have improved the job skills and knowledge base of early childhood education practitioners.

Method

Instrument

Survey of Practitioners Regarding Quality Improvement System is a survey instrument designed to gauge early childhood QIS practitioners' experiences in and reactions to QIS. This instrument contains 30 questions that collect information on QIS practitioners' background (i.e., working experience and racial-ethnic background) and their familiarity and opinion about QIS. In particular, it measures QIS practitioners' experiences in and reactions to several QIS program initiatives including (a) the early learning coaches program, (b) the career advisors program, (c) the SEEK scholarship program, (d) the workshops and conferences offered through the Registry at the Palm Beach Community College, and (e) the WAGE$ program. Major outcome measures are (a) improvement of job skills for early childhood education as perceived by QIS practitioners and (b) change of QIS practitioners in level of degree/certification in early childhood education. The survey seeks to generate data that can be used to address how various programs under QIS have impacted outcome measures.[1] The survey is designed for on-line implementation with information gathered entirely through electronic means. Survey Monkey is used as the primary software package to format the instrument (questionnaire), distribute the questionnaire to QIS practitioners, and gather data from QIS practitioners. Both pilot and formal surveys were carried out in June of 2008.

Questions in the survey were composed by a team of early childhood education experts from the Children's Services Council of Palm Beach County and external program evaluators with inputs from QIS practitioners. A pilot study was conducted after the questionnaire was finalized. Procedurally, an electronic version of the questionnaire, exactly the same to be sent out to QIS practitioners in the formal survey, was sent to five QIS practitioners chosen at random from a list of all QIS practitioners provided by the Children's Services Council of Palm Beach County. Only five QIS practitioners were asked to participate in the pilot study because the instrument aimed mainly to seek simple participation facts rather than to measure complex theoretical constructs (in the latter case a more complex pilot is desirable).[2] Apart from this field pilot study, expert opinions were also sought to improve the questionnaire. Based on both efforts, the final on-line survey instrument was made ready for implementation.

Sample

In an effort to obtain an adequate sample for data analysis, the questionnaire was sent to all QIS practitioners who had a valid e-mail address in the Registry (a database maintained by the Palm Beach Community College) considered the population of our study (N = 640). QIS practitioners had two weeks to complete the on-line questionnaire with one reminder at the end of the first week. A total of 144 QIS practitioners completed questionnaires (a return rate of 23%).[3] Among the respondents, 41% were White, 38% Black, 15% Hispanic, and 6% others. On average, they had worked in the childcare industry for 12 years and at the current childcare site for 7 years. The majority (76%) felt that they knew QIS quite well. Data gathered from this sample of QIS practitioners were cleaned and made ready for data analysis.

Analysis

One of the major outcome variables was perceived improvement of job skills measured on a 4-point Likert-type scale, and as such was considered as a continuous dependent variable. Multiple regression analysis was employed to examine the effects of various programs (early learning coaches, career advisors, SEEK scholarships, workshops and conferences offered through the Registry, and the WAGE$ program) on perceived improvement of job skills with the statistical control of QIS practitioners' background (working experience and racial-ethnic background). This statistical control was achieved by means of block entry of independent variables with background variables entered first and program variables entered thereafter. This method of block entry for multiple regression analysis is able to adequately adjust confounding factors (see Cohen & Cohen, 1983). Note that block entry was used in all subsequent statistical analyses of the survey data. Statistically significant effects would indicate significantly important program effects on perceived improvement of job skills.

Meanwhile, change in level of degree/certification in early childhood education, the other major outcome variable, was dichotomous, measuring whether change, such as that in earned academic degrees, occurs before and after QIS. The measure was based on the change along the following typology: (a) 40 Hour Certification + 5 Hour Literacy Training (30 + 5 for family childcare owners), (b) GED/HS Diploma, (c) Staff Credential, (d) Director's Credential, (e) National Credential, (f) College Credit Certificate (12 credits), (g) AS or AA degree, (h) Bachelor's Degree, and (i) Master's Degree (and beyond). Logistic regression analysis was employed to examine the effects of various programs on the likelihood of change in level of degree/certification in early childhood education occurring with the statistical control of QIS practitioners' background. Statistically significant effects would indicate significantly important program effects on change of knowledge base.

Finally examined as still another outcome measure was whether QIS practitioners stay at their current childcare facility as a result of the WAGE$ program. Because this dependent variable was also dichotomous, logistic regression analysis was employed to examine whether the WAGE$ program was capable of retaining QIS practitioners at their current childcare facility with the statistical control of QIS practitioners' background.

Results

Effects of the Early Learning Coaches Program on Perceived Improvement of Job Skills

The majority (83%) of QIS practitioners met with an early learning coach. This analysis focused on these QIS practitioners who worked with early learning coaches. The outcome measure asked these QIS practitioners about the extent to which working with early learning coaches improved the skills they use at their job (not at all, just a little, quite a bit, to a great extent). On average, they reported 24 hours of contact with early learning coaches each month for a total of 16 months. The majority (80%) reported that working with early learning coaches improved their skills used at the job either quite a bit or to a great extent.

Four multiple regression models were performed to examine absolute effects and relative effects of the early learning coaches program on perceived improvement of job skills. Models 1 and 2 examined the effects of the number of hours per month working with early learning coaches and the number of months working with early learning coaches separately for their absolute program effects. Note that the former is considered as a measure of the intensity of the program; the latter, a measure of the duration of the program. Model 3 summed the total number of hours working with early learning coaches and thus examined the total program effects. Model 4 had double functions to (a) adjust the total program effects over the intensity and duration of the program to gain insight into the relative total program effects and (b) form a complete interaction effects model given that statistically the total number of hours working with early learning coaches is calculated as the product of the number of hours per month and the number of months working with early learning coaches. All models included statistical control over background variables of QIS practitioners (see block 1).

Table 7.1 presents analytical results on the effects of the early learning coaches program on perceived improvement of job skills. Hispanic QIS practitioners benefited the most from working with early learning coaches. Across the four models, the statistically significant advantage of Hispanic over White QIS practitioners was about 25% of a standard deviation (SD) (see the β column).

Table 7.1: *Effects of Working with Early Learning Coaches on Perceived Improvement of Job Skills*

Variables	Effect	SE	β
Model 1 ($R^2 = .084$)			
Working experience (block 1)	.015	.010	.155
Black (block 1)	-.092	.183	-.056
Hispanic (block 1)	.525*	.243	.234
Others (block 1)	.348	.324	.114
A: Number of hours per month working with early learning coaches (block 2)	-.049	.243	-.021
Model 2 ($R^2 = .180$)			
Working experience (block 1)	.005	.010	.046
Black (block 1)	-.133	.173	-.076
Hispanic (block 1)	.582*	.220	.260
Others (block 1)	.480	.337	.135
B: Number of months working with early learning coaches (block 2)	.018*	.005	.336
Model 3 ($R^2 = .139$)			
Working experience (block 1)	.015	.011	.142
Black (block 1)	-.110	.202	-.061
Hispanic (block 1)	.642*	.262	.264
Others (block 1)	.490	.363	.143
A × B (block 2)	.040*	.020	.212
Model 4 ($R^2 = .167$)			
Working experience (block 1)	.011	.011	.109
Black (block 1)	-.092	.191	-.054
Hispanic (block 1)	.653*	.247	.291
Others (block 1)	.466	.342	.147
A: Number of hours per month working with early learning coaches (block 2)	.007	.369	.003
B: Number of months working with early learning coaches (block 2)	.012	.007	.236
A × B (block 2)	.013	.029	.076

Note. * $p < .05$. Effect indicates unstandardized regression coefficient. β indicates standardized regression coefficient. Number of hours per month working with early learning coaches is used with 100 hours as one measurement unit.

The number of hours per month working with early learning coaches, the measure of program intensity, had no statistically significant effects on perceived improvement of job skills (see Model 1), whereas the number of months, the measure of program duration, had statistically significant effects on perceived improvement of job skills (see Model 2). Model 2 showed that one more month of working with early learning coaches led to 34% of a SD increase in perceived improvement of job skills. A comparison of standardized regression coefficients (ßs) in Model 2 showed that the effect of program duration was larger than individual differences (racial-ethnic effects) (0.34 versus 0.26). In other words, even after adjustment over racial-ethnic differences, the duration of the early learning coaches program still had statistically significant effects on perceived improvement of job skills. This is a strong indication that early learning coaches are an effective program if in place for a sufficient period of time. The longer QIS practitioners work with early learning coaches, the more improvement of job skills they report, a finding that was corroborated by another study we conducted that focused on the pre- and post-observations using ECERS, ITERS, ECERS-R, and ITERS-R (Ma et al., 2011).

The total program effects of early learning coaches, measured by the product of the number of hours per month and the number of months working with early learning coaches (to get the total number of hours working with early learning coaches), were statistically significant (see Model 3). However, a comparison of standardized regression coefficients showed that the total program effects were not as strong as individual differences (racial-ethnic effects) (0.21 versus 0.26). The critical importance of the duration of the program was confirmed in Model 4. After control over the number of hours per month and the number of months working with early learning coaches, the total program effects disappeared. Considering this result together with earlier ones (see Models 1 and 2) indicated that the total program effects observed in Model 3 came mainly from the duration of the program.

Effects of the career advisors program on careers in early childcare

The vast majority (91%) of QIS practitioners met with a career advisor from the Palm Beach Community College. This analysis was about these QIS practitioners. The outcome measure asked these QIS practitioners the extent to which working with career advisors impacted their career in early childcare (not at all, just a little, quite a bit, to a great extent). They reported meeting with a career advisor for an average of 4 times a year and for an average of 2 years. The majority (69%) reported that the career advisors program impacted their career in early childcare either quite a bit or to a great extent.

Table 7.2: *Effects of Working with Career Advisors on Career in Early Childcare*

Variables	Effect	SE	β
Model 1 (R^2 = .153)			
Working experience (block 1)	.002	.010	.020
Black (block 1)	.570*	.180	.311
Hispanic (block 1)	.506*	.226	.212
Others (block 1)	.251	.304	.076
A: Number of times a year working with career advisors (block 2)	.039*	.015	.224
Model 2 (R^2 = .093)			
Working experience (block 1)	-.005	.010	-.048
Black (block 1)	.447*	.181	.255
Hispanic (block 1)	.415*	.227	.175
Others (block 1)	.012	.291	.004
B: Number of years working with career advisors (block 2)	.055	.041	.130
Model 3 (R^2 = .128)			
Working experience (block 1)	-.002	.010	-.017
Black (block 1)	.580*	.193	.325
Hispanic (block 1)	.474*	.225	.209
Others (block 1)	.164	.300	.053
A × B (block 2)	.006	.005	.113
Model 4 (R^2 = .187)			
Working experience (block 1)	-.001	.010	-.006
Black (block 1)	.604*	.191	.340
Hispanic (block 1)	.505*	.220	.225
Others (block 1)	.243	.293	.079
A: Number of times a year working with career advisors (block 2)	.057*	.024	.348
B: Number of years working with career advisors (block 2)	.092	.059	.226
A × B (block 2)	-.012	.009	-.238

Note. * $p < .05$. Effect indicates unstandardized regression coefficient. β indicates standardized regression coefficient.

Four multiple regression models were performed to examine absolute effects and relative effects of the career advisors program. Models 1 and 2 examined the effects of the number of times per year working with career advisors and the number of years working with career advisors separately for their absolute program effects. Similar to the case of early learning coaches, the former is considered as a measure of the intensity of the program and the latter a measure of the duration of the program. Getting the total number of times working with career advisors, Model 3 examined the absolute total program effects. Again, similar to the case of early learning coaches, Model 4 was designed to examine the relative total program effects and to form a complete interaction effects model. All models included statistical control over background variables of QIS practitioners (see block 1). Table 7.2 presents analytical results on the effects of the career advisors program on careers in early childcare among QIS practitioners.

Both Black and Hispanic QIS practitioners benefited more than White QIS practitioners from career advisors. Blacks benefited even more from the career advisors program than Hispanics. Across the four models, the statistically significant advantages over White QIS practitioners were about 30% of a SD for Blacks and about 20% of a SD for Hispanics.

The number of times per year working with career advisors, the measure of program intensity, had statistically significant effects on early childcare careers of QIS practitioners (see Model 1), whereas the number of years working with career advisors, the measure of program duration, had no statistically significant effects (see Model 2). In Model 1, one more time within a year working with career advisors increased career impact by 22% of a SD among QIS practitioners.

The total program effects of career advisors, measured by the product of the number of times per year and the number of years working with career advisors (to get the total number of times working with career advisors), were not statistically significant (see Model 3). Therefore, Models 1 to 3 highlighted the critical importance of the program intensity that was confirmed in Model 4 where the effects associated with the intensity of the career advisors program remained statistically significant even after control over the duration and total program effects and in particular the strong individual differences (racial-ethnic effects). In fact, the relative effects of the intensity of the program were just as strong as individual differences. All these results indicated that the effects of the career advisors program came from the intensity of the intervention. Overall, career advisors are a very effective program if QIS practitioners engage in frequent interactions with career advisors within a short period of time (i.e., a year). The more intensive the interactions between career advisors and QIS practitioners, the more impacts on QIS practitioners' careers in early childcare.

Effects of the SEEK scholarship program on perceived improvement of Job skills

The majority (83%) of QIS practitioners received a SEEK scholarship from the Palm Beach Community College. This analysis focused on these QIS practitioners. The outcome measure asked these QIS practitioners the degree to which they enhanced their skills in early childcare as a result of receiving the SEEK scholarship (not at all, just a little, quite a bit, to a great extent). The vast majority (92%)

indicated that the scholarship did enhance their skills in early childcare either "quite a bit" or to a "great extent".

Table 7.3: *Effects of Receiving SEEK Scholarship on Perceived Improvement of Job Skills*

Variables	Effect	SE	β
Model 1 (R^2 = .110)			
Working experience (block 1)	.002	.007	.023
Black (block 1)	.186	.126	.143
Hispanic (block 1)	.169	.169	.095
Others (block 1)	-.060	.229	-.024
Used SEEK scholarship for tuition for college courses (block 2)	.420*	.121	.308
Model 2 (R^2 = .024)			
Working experience (block 1)	.002	.007	.024
Black (block 1)	.180	.134	.138
Hispanic (block 1)	.101	.177	.057
Others (block 1)	.072	.236	.029
Used SEEK scholarship for workshop and conference (block 2)	.135	.176	.070
Model 3 (R^2 = .094)			
Working experience (block 1)	.003	.007	.041
Black (block 1)	.161	.128	.124
Hispanic (block 1)	.139	.170	.078
Others (block 1)	.057	.227	.023
Used SEEK scholarship for book and supply (block 2)	.363*	.116	.275
Model 4 (R^2 = .122)			
Working experience (block 1)	.002	.007	.029
Black (block 1)	.169	.128	.129
Hispanic (block 1)	.163	.170	.091
Others (block 1)	-.035	.231	-.014
Used SEEK scholarship for tuition for college courses (block 2)	.301	.156	.221
Used SEEK scholarship for workshop and conference (block 2)	.034	.174	.018
Used SEEK scholarship for book and supply (block 2)	.178	.152	.135

Note. * $p < .05$. Effect indicates unstandardized regression coefficient. β indicates standardized regression coefficient.

Four multiple regression models were performed to examine absolute effects and relative effects of the SEEK scholarship program on perceived improvement of job skills. Models 1 to 3 examined the effects of using SEEK scholarship for (a) tuition for college courses, (b) workshop and conference, and (c) book and supply separately for their absolute program effects. Model 4 examined the relative program effects to discern which aspect of the program has the strongest effects on perceived improvement of job skills. All models included statistical control over background variables of QIS practitioners (see block 1). Table 3 presents analytical results on the effects of the SEEK scholarship program on perceived improvement of job skills.

First of all, evident across all four models is the lack of statistically significant effects associated with QIS practitioners' background. Using SEEK scholarship for tuition for college courses showed statistically significant effects on perceived improvement of job skills (see Model 1). QIS practitioners using this option reported improvement of their job skills 31% of a SD higher than QIS practitioners avoiding this option. Using SEEK scholarship for workshop and conference showed no statistically significant effects on perceived improvement of job skills (see Model 2). Using SEEK scholarship for book and supply showed statistically significant effects on perceived improvement of job skills (see Model 3). QIS practitioners using this option reported improvement of their job skills 28% of a SD higher than QIS practitioners avoiding this option. Using SEEK scholarship for tuition for college courses showed slightly larger effects on perceived improvement of job skills than using SEEK scholarship for book and supply.

However, when all three options of using SEEK scholarship were considered together for their relative effects, no option showed statistically significant effects on improvement of job skills (see Model 4). Considering this result together with earlier findings (Models 1 to 3) suggests that using SEEK scholarship for tuition for college courses and for book and supply might share much (common) effects (so that when one is examined with the effects of the other statistically removed or statistically controlled, little unique effects remain in it). Overall, using SEEK scholarship for tuition for college courses and for book and supply turns out to be an effective way to improve job skills of QIS practitioners.

Effects of Workshops and Conferences by the Registry on Perceived Improvement of Job skills

The majority (79%) of QIS practitioners attended workshops or conferences approved and offered by the Registry at the Palm Beach Community College. This analysis was about these QIS practitioners. The outcome measure asked these QIS practitioners the extent to which their skills in early childcare were enhanced as a result of attending these workshops and conferences (not at all, just a little, quite a bit, to a great extent). They attended, on average, 5 conferences or workshops, and the majority (89%) indicated that the workshops or conferences enhanced their skills in early childcare either quite a bit or to a great extent.

One multiple regression model was run to examine whether attendance to workshops and conferences offered or approved by the Registry was associated with perceived improvement of job skills among QIS practitioners (see Table 7.4). There were statistically significant effects associated with attendance at Registry-approved workshops and conferences. Attending one more Registry-approved workshop or conference led to an increase of 24% of a SD in perceived improvement of job skills. Therefore, Registry-approved workshops and conferences are effective in improving job skills of QIS practitioners. The more Registry-approved workshops and conferences QIS practitioners attend, the greater the improvement of job skills they report.

Table 7.4: *Effects of Attending Workshops and Conferences on Perceived Improvement of Job Skills*

Variables	Effect	SE	β
Model 1 ($R^2 = .119$)			
Working experience (block 1)	-.009	.009	-.105
Black (block 1)	.238	.161	.161
Hispanic (block 1)	.418	.226	.195
Others (block 1)	-.228	.281	-.083
Number of attended workshops and conferences (block 2)	.040*	.017	.235

Note. * $p < .05$. Effect indicates unstandardized regression coefficient. β indicates standardized regression coefficient.

Effects of the WAGE$ Program on Decision to Stay at Current Facility

The majority (53%) of QIS practitioners utilized the WAGE$ program. This analysis focused on these QIS practitioners. The outcome measure asked these QIS practitioners whether the WAGE$ program helped them to stay at their current childcare facility or site (yes or no). Nearly half (48%) indicated that the WAGE$ program did help them to stay.

One logistic regression model was run to examine whether utilizing the WAGE$ program helps QIS practitioners to stay at the current facility (see Table 7.5). Utilizing the WAGE$ program had statistically significant effects on QIS practitioners' decision to stay at the current facility. In fact, QIS practitioners who utilized the WAGE$ program were 1.33 times as likely to stay at their current facilities than QIS practitioners who did not utilize the program. Therefore, the WAGE$ program is effective in helping QIS practitioners to stay at their current facility.

Table 7.5: *Effects of Participating in WAGE$ Program on Decision to Stay at Current Facility*

Variables	Effect	SE	Exp
Model 1 (Nagelkerke $R^2 = 0.072$)			
Working experience	-0.030	0.035	0.971
Black (block 1)	0.995	0.567	2.704
Hispanic (block 1)	0.586	0.695	1.797
Others (block 1)	0.054	1.090	1.055
Intercept (measuring effects of utilizing the WAGE$ program)	0.282*	0.586	1.326

Note. * $p < .05$. Exp denotes *e* raised to the power of the effect, often referred to as odds ratio. Out of 76 early childhood practitioners who have utilized the WAGE$ program, 45 report effects on decision to stay at current facility whereas 29 report no effects on decision to stay at current facility (2 provide no responses).

Effects of Programs on Change in Level of Certification or Degree in Early Childhood Care and Education

This outcome measure examined if there were changes in level of certification or degree in early childcare education before and after taking part in various programs in QIS. The majority (56%) of QIS practitioners reported a change in certification or degree after participation in QIS. Table 7.6 shows results from one logistic regression model that was run to examine whether various programs (the WAGE$ program, early learning coaches, career advisors, workshops and conferences, and college course credits) had any effects on change in the level of certification or degree before and after QIS. First of all, there were statistically significant individual differences. Less experienced QIS practitioners were more likely to pursue change in the level of certification or degree than more experienced QIS practitioners. QIS practitioners with one less year of working experience were 1.20 times as likely to pursue change in the level of certification or degree (1 (0.84). White QIS practitioners were more likely to pursue change in the level of certification or degree than both Black QIS practitioners (1 (0.08 = 13 times as likely) and Hispanic QIS practitioners (1 (0.09 = 12 times as likely).

Table 7.6: *Effects of Participating in WAGE$ Program, Early Learning Coaches, Career Advisors, Workshops and Conferences, and College Course Credits on Change in Level of Certification or Degree*

Variables	Effect	SE	Exp
Model 1 (Nagelkerke R^2 = .566)			
Working experience (block 1)	-.180*	.079	.836
Black (block 1)	-2.590*	1.249	.075
Hispanic (block 1)	-2.454	1.544	.086
Utilizing WAGE$ program (block 2)	.727	.981	2.069
Number of hours working with early learning coaches (block 2)	.015	.101	1.015
Number of times working with career advisors (block 2)	-.029	.026	.971
Number of attended workshops and conferences by the Registry (block 2)	-.048	.107	.954
Number of college course credits earned with the support of QIS (block 2)	.148*	.073	1.160

Note. * $p < .05$. Exp denotes e raised to the power of the effect, often referred to as odds ratio. Number of hours working with early learning coaches is used with 100 hours as one measurement unit.

Among all programs, only college course credits were statistically significantly associated with change in the level of certification or degree. One more college course credit increased the chance of a change in the level of certification or degree by a factor of 1.16 times. Therefore, the accumulation of sufficient college course credits leads to a substantial chance of an improvement in the level of certification or degree. From this perspective, encouraging QIS practitioners to pursue college course credits is a very effective strategy to improve QIS practitioners' level of certification or degree.

Discussion

Principal Findings

Data analysis on the basis of the Survey of Practitioners Regarding Quality Improvement System has revealed many interesting findings on early childhood education practitioners' experiences in and reactions to various programs embedded in QIS. Principal findings of data analysis include that (a) the duration, rather than the intensity, of the early learning coaches program is associated with perceived improvement of job skills of QIS practitioners; (b) the intensity, rather than the duration, of the career advisors program is associated with impact on QIS practitioners' career; (c) with respect to perceived improvement of job skills of QIS practitioners, the most effective aspects of SEEK scholarship emphasized the utilization of the scholarship for (i) tuition for college courses and (ii) book and supply, two aspects that shared much (common) program effects; (d) workshops and conferences approved by the Palm Beach County Registry, rather than any workshops and conferences, were an effective way to improve job skills of QIS practitioners, a finding that indicates the importance of the quality of professional development activities; (e) the WAGE$ program was effective in helping QIS practitioners to stay at their current facility; (f) among all programs implemented in QIS, encouraging QIS practitioners to pursue college course credits was the most effective in improving their certification or degree level in early childhood education; and (g) there were differential impacts on White practitioners and their Black and Hispanic counterparts. Based on these principal findings, we elaborate on a number of implications that aim to inform educational policy and practice.

Duration and Intensity of Professional Development Programs

In our study, early learning coaches and career advisors are among the most important factors in the career development of early childhood education practitioners. The major elements of this kind of interactive programs are duration (how long to interact) and intensity (how often to interact). We found that duration, rather than intensity, matters for coaches to help practitioners improve their job skills. In other words, coaches need sufficient time to impact job skills of practitioners. Our finding is consistent with the increasing literature concluding that the profession al development program has to be sustained to be effective. Therefore, the most effective way to improve job skills of practitioners is for them to develop a long-term partnership with coaches. Policymakers and administrators need to make efforts to financially sustain early learning coaches program for a sufficient period of time. A compensation structure for coaches and a reward structure for practitioners are critical to sustain such a long-term commitment.

On the other hand, we found that intensity, rather than duration, matters for career advisors to impact early childhood education practitioners' careers. Stated differently, advisors need to interact frequently with practitioners to advise on their career issues. Therefore, the most effective way to impact the career path of practitioners is for them to engage in intensive short-term guidance and consultation with advisors, particularly during the initial years of their careers when practitioners are most likely to leave their profession. Policymakers and administrators in this case need to provide resources and opportunities for an intensive interaction between advisors and practitioners. Compensating advisors and allowing working with advisors as a part of paid duty (e.g., paid professional development) for practitioners are important to encourage such an intensive upfront commitment.

The Quality of Courses, Workshops, and Conferences

One important finding of the present research is the convergence of courses, workshops, and conferences in terms of their effects on improving job skills of early childhood education practitioners. In other words, continuing education or training is a critical measure to improve job skills of practitioners. Even using SEEK scholarship to purchase books and supplies significantly helped practitioners perceive improvement in their job skills. Since books and supplies were purchased for the purpose of attending courses, this aspect of scholarship becomes a part of the convergence. However, our research found that althoughworkshops and conferences approved by Palm Beach County Registry were effective in improving job skills of QIS practitioners, other workshops and conferences were not. The Palm Beach County Registry has a set of criteria for approving workshops and conferences. Therefore, it is important to have quality control measures for developing and offering a professional development program.

This strong impact of attending courses, workshops, and conferences on the perceived improvement of job skills among early childhood education practitioners makes us think about potential policy implications that take advantage of this strong program effect. We believe that a part-time program that allows the accumulation of course credits toward a certificate, a bachelor's or even a master's degree can serve the purposes of improving job skills, knowledge base, and the level of certification or degree of practitioners. In fact, we emphasize that pursuing college course credits was found in the present research as the most effective way to improve practitioners' certification or degree levels in early childhood care and education.

Obviously, such a part-time program should be cost effective to run and should attract a large number of practitioners with its flexibility in credit building. Apart from formal college courses that warrant quality of training, the Palm Beach Community College has already reviewed and approved informal workshops and conferences that are of quality. With all these potential features of and existing efforts toward such a part-time program, policymakers and administrators are in a win-win position to put this concept into practice with minor impact on budget but major impact on improvement of practitioners in terms of job skills, knowledge base, and the level of certification or degree in early childhood care and education.

Prevention of Attrition

As we discussed earlier, the WAGE$ program was designed to prevent attrition of early childhood education practitioners, and we did find that the WAGE$ program was effective in helping practitioners stay at their current facility. Obviously, professionals are less likely to leave their profession if they are paid more. Although the WAGE$ program was a temporary measure for prevention of attrition, we seek policy implications that may come from this strong program effect. With the recognition of salary gaps in society, we recommend that policymakers and administrators may provide "indirect WAGE$." For example, improving job benefits and even providing a certain form of housing credits can become measures to retain practitioners.

Differential Impacts on Practitioners of Various Racial and Ethnic Groups

Our results indicated that in comparison to their White counterparts, Hispanic practitioners benefited the most from early learning coaches, and both Black and Hispanic practitioners benefited more from career advisors. However, Black and Hispanic practitioners were less likely to report an improvement in level of degree or certification in early child care and education than their White counterparts. There might be more barriers for Black and Hispanic practitioners in terms of educational preparation and financial resources. However, as far as policy is concerned, more encouragement and support, from both quality and quantity perspectives, should be given to minority practitioners to engage in professional development and pursue advancement in certification and degree levels.

Coda

Based on our research we have some significant findings that point to the effective elements of a quality improvement system of early care and education. Among others, we found that (a) the duration of early learning coaching, (b) the intensity of career advisors, (c) quality workshops and conferences, (d) college courses, and (e) scholarships for books and supplies in relation to taking college courses are effective for improving practitioners' job skills and level of certification and degree in early childhood care and education. We found that additional income to practitioners through the WAGE$ program is effective in retaining them. We also found that the professional development program has a differential impact on practitioners of various racial and ethnic groups and that more encouragement and support should be given to Black and Hispanic practitioners to engage in professional development and pursue advancement in the level of certificate and degree. All these findings have implications for the policy of early care and education in general and for other quality improvement initiatives for early care and education in particular.

Notes

1. For a complete version of the survey questionnaire, please refer to Appendix H. in the On-line Survey Questionnaire for Practitioners in the full evaluation report (Shen, Tackett, & Ma, 2008) retrievable at http://cache.trustedpartner.com/docs/library/000238/ECEQISEvaluation2008.pdf.
2. For exactly the same reason, we did not perform any psychometric analysis on the pilot data. In general, psychometric analysis is often necessary for instruments aimed to measure complex theoretical constructs (e.g., attitude, motivation) but is often unnecessary for instruments aimed to collect simple information (simple participation facts in our case).
3. Even though some researchers may consider this return rate rather low, it is not a major concern in our research. We defined all QIS practitioners (N = 640) in the Registry database as our population, and we treated QIS practitioners who returned our questionnaires as a sample for data analysis. Of course, this sample was a volunteering sample. Like many studies that employ volunteering samples, generalization of analytical results to our population needs caution.

References

Barnett, W. S. (1995). Long-term effects of early childhood programs on cognitive and school outcomes. In R. E. Behrman (ed.), *Long-term outcomes of early childhood programs* (pp. 25–50). Princeton, NJ: Center for the Future of Children.

Belfield, C. R. (2004). *Early education: How important are the cost savings to the school system?* New York: Teachers College.

Bredekamp, S., & Copple, C. (Eds.). (1997). *Developmentally appropriate practice in early childhood programs* (rev. ed.). Washington, DC: National Association for the Education of Young Children.

Children's Forum. (2011). *Miami-Date County Quality Counts workforce study.* Tallahassee, Florida: Children's Forum.

Ciyer, A., Nagasawa, M., Swadener, B. B., & Patet, P. (2010). Impacts of the Arizona System Ready/Child Ready Professional Development Project on preschool teachers' self-efficacy. *Journal of Early Childhood Teacher Education, 31* (2), 129–145

Cohen, J., & Cohen, P. (1983). *Applied multiple regression/correlation analysis in behavioral sciences* (2nd ed.). Hillsdale, NJ: Erlbaum.

Committee on Integrating the Science of Early Childhood Development. (2000). *From neurons to neighborhoods: The science of early childhood development.* Washington, DC: National Academy Press.

Currie, J. (2000, May). *Early childhood intervention programs: What do we know?* Paper presented at a research briefing on Early Childhood Intervention Programs: Are the Costs Justified? Washington, DC: Subcommittee of Human Resources of the U.S. House of Representatives Committee on Ways and Means & Joint Center for Poverty Research.

Entwisle, D. R. (1995). The role of schools in sustaining early childhood program benefits. In R. E. Behrman (ed.), *Long-term outcomes of early childhood programs* (pp. 133–160). Princeton, NJ: Center for the Future of Children.

Espinosa, L. M. (2008). *Challenging common myths about young English language learners.* New York: Foundation for Child Development.

Friendly, M., Doherty, G., & Beach, J. (2006). *Quality by design: What do we know about quality in early learning and child care, and what do we think? A literature review.* Toronto, Canada: Childcare Resource and Research Unit, University of Toronto.

Greene, W. (2006). Universal preschool: A costly but worthy goal. *Journal of Law and Education, 35,* 555–563.

Hamre, B., Pianta, R., & Downer, J. (2009). *Supporting language and literacy development in preschool classrooms through effective teacher-child interactions.* Poster presented at the Institute of Education Sciences Research Conference, Washington, DC.

Hart, C., Burts, D., & Charlesworth, R. (1997). Integrated developmentally appropriate curriculum: From theory and research to practice. In C. Hart, D. Burts, & R. Charlesworth (Eds.), *Integrated curriculum and developmentally appropriate practice: Birth to age eight* (pp. l–27). Buffalo, NY: SUNY Press.

Isner, T., Tout, K., Zaslow, M., Soli, M., Quinn, K., Rothenberg., L., & Burkhauser, M. (2011). *Coaching in early care and education programs and Quality Rating and Improvement Systems (QRIS); Identifying promising features. Report produced for Children's Services Council of Palm Beach County.* Washington, DC: Child Trends.

Kagan, S. L., & Kauerz, K. (2006). Preschool programs: Effective curricula. In R. E. Tremblay, R. G. Barr, & R. V. Peters (Eds.). *Encyclopedia on early childhood development.* Montreal, Canada: Centre of Excellence for Early Childhood Development.

Katz, L. G. (1993). Multiple perspectives on the quality of early childhood programmes. *European Early Childhood Education Research Journal, 1*(2), 5–10.

Landry, S. H., Anthony, J. L., Swank, P. R.; & Monseque-Bailey, P. (2009). Effectiveness of comprehensive professional development for teachers of at-risk preschoolers. *Journal of Educational Psychology, 101* (2), 448–465.

Ludwig, J. & Sawhill, I. (2007). *Success by ten: Intervening early, often and effectively in the education of young children.* Washington, DC: Brookings Institute.

Lynch, R. (2004). *Exceptional returns: Economic, fiscal and social benefits of investment in early childhood development.* Washington, DC: Economic Policy Development Institute.

Ma, X., Shen, J., Kavanaugh, A., Lu, X., Brandi, K., Goodman, J., Till, L., & Watson, G. (2011). Effects of quality improvement system on child care centers. *Journal of Research in Childhood Education, 25,* (4) 399–414

Maxwell, K. L., & Clifford, R. M. (2006). Professional development issues in universal prekindergarten. In E. Zigler, W. Gilliam, & S. M. Jones (Eds.), *A vision of universal preschool education.* (pp. 169–193). New York: Cambridge University Press

National Research Council. (1999). *Starting out right.* Washington, DC: National Academy Press.

Nelson, A. (2006). Closing the gap: Early childhood education. *Info Brief, 45,* 1–8.

Neuman, S. B., & Cunningham, L. (2009). The impact of professional development and coaching on early language and literacy instructional practices. *American Educational Research Journal, 46* (2), 532–566.

NICHD Early Child Care Research Network (2002). Structure, process, outcome: Direct and indirect effects of caregiving quality on young children's development. *Psychological Science, 13*(3), *199–206.*

Pianta, R.C., Mashburn, A. J., Downer, J.T., Hamre, B.K., & Justice, L. (2008). Effects of web-mediated professional development resources on teacher-child interactions in pre-kindergarten classrooms. *Early Childhood Research Quarterly, 23,* 431–45.

Pittard, M., Zaslow, M., Lavelle, B., & Porter, T. (2006). *Investing in quality: A survey of state child care and development fund initiatives.* Washington, DC & New York: National Association of State Child Care Administrators, the Bank Street College of Education, & Child Trends.

Ramey, C. T., & Ramey, S. L. (1998). Prevention of intellectual disabilities: Early interventions to improve cognitive development. *Preventive Medicine, 27,* 224–232.

Saracho, O. N., & Spodek, B. (2007). Early childhood teacher's preparation and the quality of program outcomes. *Early Childhood Development and Care, 1,* 71–91.

Schweinhart, L. J., Barnes, H. V., & Weikart, D. P. (1993). *Significant benefits: The High/Scope Perry Preschool Study through age 27.* Ypsilanti, MI: High/Scope Press.

Shen, J, Ma, X., & Tackett, W. (2009). *Second year evaluation report for Palm Beach County Quality Improvement System.* Palm Beach, FL: Children 's Services Council of Palm Beach County.

Shen, J, Tackett, W., & Ma, X. (2008). *First year evaluation report for Palm Beach County Quality Improvement System.* Palm Beach, FL: Children 's Services Council of Palm Beach County.

Stipek, D. J., & Byler, P. (1997). Early childhood education teachers: Do they practice what they preach? *Early Childhood Research Quarterly, 12,* 305–325.

Takanishi, R., & Kauerz, K. (2008). PK inclusion: Getting serious about a P-16 education system. *Phi Delta Kappa, 89,* 480–487.

Tout, K., Zaslow, M. & Berry, D. (2006). Quality and qualifications: Links between professional development and quality in early care and education settings. In Zaslow, M. & Martinez-Beck, I. (Eds.), *Critical issues in early childhood professional development* (pp. 77–110). Baltimore: Brookes Publishing.

University of Pittsburgh Office of Child Development & Pennsylvania State University Prevention Research Center. (2006). *Evaluation of Pennsylvania's Keystone STARS Quality Rating System in child care settings.* Pennsylvania: University of Pittsburgh Office of Child Development.

Waldfogel, J. (2002). Child care, women's employment and child outcomes. *Journal of Population Economics, 15,* 527–548.

8

Effects of Quality Improvement System on Childcare Centers

XIN MA, JIANPING SHEN, AMY KAVANAUGH, XUEJIN LU, KAREN BRANDI, JEFF GOODMAN, LANCE TILL, AND GRACE WATSON

Introduction

Quality early childhood care and education where children participate in developmentally appropriate programs can make a difference in academic achievement, social adjustment, and school graduation (Campbell, Ramey, Pungello, Sparling, & Miller-Johnson, 2002; Espinosa, 2008; Shlay, Tran, Weinraub, & Harmon, 2005). It reduces the likelihood of grade retention or placement in special education (Currie, 2001). It is important to young English language learners for academic excellence (Espinosa, 2008). The negative effects of poverty can be compensated by participation in quality early childhood education programs (Dahlberg & Moss, 2005). Early childhood education is a solid foundation for preschool to college education (P-16), promoting educational excellence, lifelong learning, and competitiveness in the job market (Takanishi & Kauerz, 2008).

State childcare agencies set general goals to ensure healthy childcare environments, provide formal training and education for providers of programs, and establish professional development systems (Pittard, Zaslow, Lavelle, & Porter, 2006). To coordinate efforts across states, the National Association for the Education of Young Children (NAEYC) developed a voluntary accreditation system for early childhood education programs in 1985 that has evolved into professional preparation standards at three levels (associate degree, initial licensure, and advanced level). Professional preparation standards are important because the level and type of education of early childhood education practitioners are critical factors in determining the quality of programs (Saracho & Spodek, 2007). The next step is to ensure that states use these established national standards to improve early childhood care and education. NAEYC advocates a systematic approach referred to as Quality Rating and Improvement System (QRIS) or Quality Improvement System (QIS) for simplicity (i.e., these two terms are interchangeable). Local authorities pursuing QIS must emphasize the two key elements of any QIS—quality rating and quality information leading to quality improvement.

Palm Beach County in Florida has designed and implemented its QIS as a system level initiative to prepare children to be healthy and ready to learn when it is time for schooling.[1] Local early childhood education advocates worked for a year to design this comprehensive, voluntary, early care and education improvement system that aims to improve the quality of childcare from birth to age five. Based on the results of a pilot program (Picower Quality Child Care Initiative), Palm Beach County finalized the goals of QIS as (a) producing positive outcomes for children; (b) providing consumer education for parents; and (c) defining, advocating for, and obtaining the resources necessary to encourage, support, and promote quality early care and education.

QIS contains six components. *Pathways to quality* emphasizes environment, professional development, staff to child ratio, management, parental involvement, curriculum, and child development screening. *Achievable standards* provides a fair system for rating a childcare site and develops a roadmap for achieving high quality. *Star ratings* indicates to what extent a childcare site has met quality criteria. *Reliable assessments* ensures a fair, consistent, and accurate assessment process for each childcare site by adopting nationally recognized, research based, assessment tools to evaluate the quality of childcare sites. *Quality improvement supports* provides financial and technical supports to childcare sites and their staff. *Consumer education opportunities* informs parents and staff of a childcare site's commitment to quality.[2]

Implementation came after design. QIS targeted 7,015 licensed childcare sites; school based childcare sites, and family childcare homes that hold a rate agreement with the county to accept children receiving subsidies. All sites were invited to participate in QIS, and 150 sites volunteered. QIS started in 2002. Sites were funded at a higher level during the first year (the intensive phase) and continued to receive services during the maintenance phase as long as they chose to remain in QIS (most sites did remain). With no funding from the state, Palm Beach

County initiated a property tax to fund QIS. Palm Beach County's Children's Services Council was in charge of QIS from design to implementation.[3]

Participating centers took part in a range of QIS programs. Star rating program assesses outcomes of children (with an emphasis on school readiness) and centers (with an emphasis on caring and learning environments) for quality improvement. Early learning coaches program and career advisors program pair early childhood practitioners with coaches to form training mentorship and with advisors to provide career guidance. Coaches and advisors first receive intensive trainings on curriculum, child development as well as coaching and advising skills. During the intensive phase, coaches and advisors work with all staff in a participating center. During the maintenance phase, coaches and advisors work more specifically with selected staff to ensure an overall quality of training and advising (selection is based on suggestions of center directors and results of staff assessments).

The Registry at Palm Beach Community College approves and offers workshops and conferences for practitioners to earn credits toward certificate and degree. Staff in all QIS centers are required to become members of the Registry and keep their individual education records current and accurate. Apart from workshops and conferences it offers, the Registry also accepts other informal and formal trainings for professional development credits required of all staff. Informal training must be approved by the Registry according to established standards. SEEK (Seek Excellence in Education and Knowledge) scholarship program allocates funds for practitioners to pursue formal continuing education. Open to all members of the Registry on a first come, first served basis, the scholarship covers textbooks and fees associated with college enrollment. WAGE$ program provides financial support to retain practitioners in the profession. Funded by the Children's Services Council of Palm Beach County and administered through the Institute of Excellence, the award is based on educational achievement and longevity. Career advisors provide practitioners with information on the program and help them with applications.

Review of Research Literature

Childcare quality is multidimensional with structure and process components (Marshall, 2004).[4] The structure component alludes to group size, staff to child ratio, staff training and education, curriculum, and physical environment (Li-Grining & Coley, 2006; Sachs, 2000). The process component pertains to social and instructional interactions between children and staff that are linked to future learning behaviors (Pianta, 2007; Wiltz & Klein, 2001). Parental perception is another dimension of quality as parents evaluate type, flexibility, affordability, and communication of a childcare site when choosing early care and education (Rudd, Cain, & Saxon, 2008).

Numerous studies converge to a conclusion that quality of childcare makes a difference in children's academic (cognitive) and social (emotional) development, even though researchers do not define quality in the same way. For example, quality pertains to classroom instruction (Curby et al., 2009), care structure such as staff education, group size, and care environment (American Educational Research Association, 2005; National Institute of Child Health and Human Development, 2003), care process such as interaction and relationship (Ahn & Stifter, 2006; Burchinal, Peisner-Feinberg, Pianta, & Howes, 2002; Rudd et al., 2008), parental perception (Shlay et al., 2005), and sensitive, adequate responses to children's social and emotional development, not just their academic advancement (Shonkoff & Phillips, 2000).

Some factors predict quality of childcare. At the child level, with an emphasis on care structure as quality measures (in relation to socioeconomic status, SES), Hynes and Habasevich-Brooks (2008) reported that families with higher incomes are more likely to participate in high quality childcare. At the site level, Sachs (2000) predicted care process (as measures of quality) from care structure, arguing that low quality childcare is more likely associated with higher staff to child ratio, staff with less education, and lower staff wages.

Consistent efforts have been directed to improve (multidimensional) quality of childcare over the past two decades, initiated by the NAEYC voluntary accreditation system (discussed earlier). The 1990 Child Care and Development Block Grant encouraged states to expand efforts to improve access to and quality of childcare (e.g., statewide planning for improvement, licensing and monitoring childcare sites, training staff, and improving access for low SES families) (see Cohen & Lord, 2005). Examples include developing a tiered rating system tied to state funding in Kentucky, establishing a star rating quality system in North Carolina, and improving staff to child ratio in Tennessee. Research synthesis revealed considerable variation among states in terms of populations served, financing of childcare, administration of grants, and use of its quality set-asides (Cohen & Lord, 2005).

Another strategy for childcare quality improvement (care process improvement) is to form partnerships with parents. Examples include personalizing interactions between staff and parents. An advocate teacher is "responsible for a small group of children for the purpose of observing development and building relationships with the parents and family" so that parents feel that teachers really know their children through specific feedback on their children (Huber, 2003, p. 75). In their systematic review of literature, Rous, Hallam, Grove, Robinson, and Machara (2003) stated that parent involvement in early care and education programs is very critical because it allows parents and providers to develop a collaborative relationship with children's needs as the focus.

Efforts to improve conditions and images of the childcare profession is another strategy to improve childcare quality (improve care structure). Examples include reducing staff turnover, increasing staff wages, advancing staff education, and improving parental perception of childcare sites. Staff are assigned to the same age group in the same classroom to improve their job satisfaction, and novice and experienced staff are also placed together for support and dialogue about classroom practice (Uttley & Horm, 2008). Downer, Kraft-Sayre, and Pianta (2009) placed a special focus on professional development of staff on the issue of interactions between staff and children.

Major challenges to achieve quality childcare include staff education and staff pay. American Association of Colleges of Teacher Education (2004) reported that they have less education and earn lower pay than their K-12 (kindergarten to high school) counterparts. The level of staff education is linked to the level of academic achievement (e.g., mathematics achievement) of pre-kindergarten children (Early, Bryant, & Pianta, 2006). The need for highly qualified staff continues to increase (Isenberg & Renck-Jalongo, 2003). Another challenge is to maintain a sufficient level of funding for childcare (Ewen, 2005). This challenge is particularly pressing for infant and toddler care (Paulsell, Nogales, & Cohen, 2003).

This research comes at a time when QRIS is getting national attention as one of the responses to those challenges (Zellman & Perlman, 2007). As many local authorities are considering their own QRIS, we provide an evaluative approach for examining the effects of these initiatives on childcare centers. This research was part of a comprehensive external evaluation of the Palm Beach County QIS, with a focus on childcare centers. It was designed to seek empirical evidence to address the first component of the Palm Beach County QIS (pathways to quality). Our research question was whether participation in QIS programs (designed to improve pathways to quality) was able to significantly improve the quality of childcare centers over several years of implementation. The definition of quality is a center-level one, alluding to the characteristics of a center's caring and learning environment.

Method

Sample and Instrument

Designed to gauge quality indicators of group programs, Early Childhood Environmental Rating Scale (ECERS) evaluates childcare centers serving children from age two and half to five, whereas Infant/Toddler Environmental Scale (ITERS) evaluates childcare centers serving children from birth to age two and half.[5] As the chief agency in charge of QIS, Children's Services Council of Palm Beach County collected and housed both ECERS and ITERS data as quality indicators of centers. Ten professionally trained assessors were used to rate classrooms with either ECERS or ITERS. The classroom was the measurement unit of both ECERS and ITERS. With a total of close to 900 classrooms, it was difficult to employ multiple assessors to every classroom. Our strategy was to send multiple assessors to a randomly selected number of classrooms to examine the issue of measurement accuracy. Inter-rater agreement was above 0.90 across all classrooms. Furthermore, in almost all cases, the same assessor evaluated all classrooms of a center as another way to control subjective biases. Part of the resulting database contained ECERS assessment records from 84 centers and ITERS assessment records from 47 centers. As reported earlier, these centers were voluntary ones that accepted an invitation (from Children's Services Council) to participate in QIS. Because the center was the evaluative unit in QIS, multiple assessment records within a center were integrated so that each center had only one record on each quality indicator.

Both ECERS and ITERS went through revisions during the implementation of QIS. QIS first used ECERS and ITERS in 2002. The revised ECERS (ECERS-R) was implemented in 2005 and the revised ITERS (ITERS-R) was implemented in 2006. With deletion and addition of items, ECERS and ECERS-R (ITERS and ITERS-R) need to be psychometrically equated to allow direct comparison of scores obtained from both scales. The fact that ECERS and ECERS-R (ITERS and ITERS-R) were not equated (so not comparable) dictated the procedure of data analysis for this research (see discussion later). The revision of instrument often raises a concern about assessor variation in that potential differences, say, between ECERS and ECERS-R may come as a result of using two different groups of assessors. To avoid this concern, assessors were kept the same for both ECERS and ECERS-R. In total, 43 items in ECERS-R and 39 items in ITERS-R are organized into seven common scales: (a) space and furnishing, (b) personal care routines, (c) language reasoning, (d) activities, (e) interactions, (f) program structure, and (g) parents and staff (QIS did not use this scale). Thus, each instrument generated data on six scales that were also integrated to generate an overall measure on the quality of a center.

Design and Analysis

The assessment of QIS childcare centers using ECERS and ITERS was carried out in a pre- and post-research design. For each center, pre-assessment generated baseline data and post-assessment generated formal data. QIS started in 2002, and centers kept entering QIS from 2002 to 2007 (all centers received the same programs). Baseline data were collected as soon as a center entered QIS, and formal data were collected 13 months later (to give the center sufficient time to receive the programs). Because ECERS and ECERS-R are not comparable, we separated the database into two parts based on the implementation date of ECERS-R in April 2005: records collected (a) before and (b) after April 2005. Similarly, we separated the database into two parts based on the implementation date of ITERS-R in April 2006: records collected (a) before and (b) after April 2006. The analyses were carried out separately for ECERS, ECERS-R, ITERS, and ITERS-R.

Analysis took the form of repeated measures models with F test that compared baseline data with formal data to discover whether there was statistically significant improvement from baseline assessment to formal assessment in term of the six indicators of early childcare programs (plus the combined overall measure of quality). Effect sizes were provided for cross-indicator comparisons to discover the indicators that showed the largest improvements. Statistical powers were also calculated to indicate how sensitively repeated measures models detected statistically significant improvements.

Of particular interest was the issue about the timing of entering QIS. A variable labeled as "year of entry" was created to denote the year when a center's baseline measure was obtained. Because the goal was to examine whether the year of entry was significantly related to the improvement from baseline measure to formal measure, there was a need to focus on centers with both measures. Although the database contained ECERS records of 84 centers, 42 had valid ECERS baseline data, and 45 had valid ECERS formal data with 41 having data from both assessments. Meanwhile, 36 centers had valid ECERS-R baseline data, and 66 centers had valid ECERS-R formal data with 18 having data from both assessments. Some centers left QIS during a period of 13 months after pre-measure (these centers did not have post-measure). Because of the instrument revision, some centers had ECERS as pre-measure but ECERS-R as post-measure. These centers possessed invalid assessments. Therefore, 59 centers were involved in a multiple regression analysis that examined the effects of year of entry on gain scores in various indicators from baseline measure to formal measure. A dummy variable was also used in this multiple regression analysis to denote type of instrument (ECERS or ECERS-R). As a result, the effects of year of entry on gain scores were actually estimated with statistical control over type of instrument employed. This adjustment was critical to ensure that the effects of type of instrument did not confound with the effects of year of entry.

In terms of ITERS, the database contained 47 centers, 24 had valid ITERS baseline data and 7 had valid ITERS formal data with 4 having data from both assessments. Meanwhile, 20 centers had valid ITERS-R baseline data and 34 centers had valid ITERS-R formal data with 9 having data from both assessments. Some centers did not have valid data for the same reasons as discussed above. Therefore, 13 centers were involved in the same multiple regression analysis as in the case of ECERS. Different in the case of ITERS was the small sample of centers involved in the multiple regression analysis.

Results

Improvement Between Baseline Assessment and Formal Assessment

Analyses of ECERS and ECERS-R scores via descriptive and inferential comparisons between baseline assessment and formal assessment helped discern whether childcare centers improved the quality of early childhood education. A descriptive comparison of means between baseline assessment and formal assessment showed little substantial changes among most quality indicators (see Table 8.1). Descriptive conclusions were confirmed in inferential comparisons. Centers evaluated with ECERS demonstrated statistically significant improvement only in one quality indicator, activities. Centers significantly improved activities they offered to children during a period of 13 months (from baseline assessment to formal assessment). The effect size of this improvement, however, was small with a magnitude of 0.13. According to Rosenthal and Rosnow (1984), effect sizes more than 0.50 are large, between 0.30 and 0.50 are moderate, and less than 0.30 are small in behavioral sciences. Repeated measures models were marginal in statistical power, with the single statistically significant result showing a power of 0.65.

Table 8.1: *Results of Comparison Between Baseline Assessment and Formal Assessment Measures Based on Early Childhood Environment Rating Scale (ECERS; Before April 2005)*

	Baseline		Formal				
Measure	*M*	*SD*	*M*	*SD*	*F*	ES	Power
Overall measure	4.97	0.93	4.93	0.58	0.11	0.00	0.06
Space and furnishing	4.79	0.99	4.49	0.72	3.15	0.07	0.41
Personal care routines	3.11	0.99	2.97	0.69	0.70	0.02	0.13
Language–reasoning	5.87	1.03	5.91	0.74	0.04	0.00	0.06
Activities	5.65	1.05	6.06	0.65	5.74*	0.13	0.65
Interaction	4.90	1.43	4.59	1.44	1.43	0.03	0.21
Program structure	5.75	1.19	5.54	0.85	1.28	0.03	0.20

Note. * $p < 0.05$. *M* = mean. *SD* = standard deviation. ES = effect size.

Table 8.2: *Results of Comparison Between Baseline Assessment and Formal Assessment Measures Based on Revised Early Childhood Environment Rating Scale (ECERS-R; April 2005 to Present)*

	Baseline		Formal				
Measure	*M*	*SD*	*M*	*SD*	*F*	ES	Power
Overall measure	3.35	0.84	4.70	0.56	34.19*	0.67	1.00
Space and furnishing	2.87	0.88	3.67	0.45	12.59*	0.43	0.92
Personal care routines	2.09	0.64	2.81	0.73	12.59*	0.43	0.92
Language–reasoning	4.26	1.19	5.92	0.78	24.18*	0.59	1.00
Activities	3.70	0.96	5.98	0.66	76.57*	0.82	1.00
Interaction	3.72	1.05	4.94	1.18	11.33*	0.40	0.89
Program structure	4.07	1.20	5.16	0.72	10.07*	0.37	0.85

Note. * $p < 0.05$. *M* = mean. *SD* = standard deviation. ES = effect size.

On the other hand, Table 8.2 indicates that centers evaluated with ECERS-R significantly improved the quality of their programs across all quality indicators during a period of 13 months (from baseline assessment to formal assessment). In fact, improvement was considerable. Space and furnishing, personal care routines, interaction, and program structure (in this order) showed moderate improvement with effect size ranging from 0.43 to 0.37. Activities and language reasoning (in this order) showed large improvement with effect size of 0.82 and 0.59. The largest improvement occurred in activities, whereas the smallest improvement occurred in program structure. The overall measure indicated that centers evaluated with ECERS-R experienced large improvement in quality with effect size of 0.67 during the period of 13 months. Repeated measures models showed high statistical power for detecting differences between baseline assessment and formal assessment.

Centers evaluated with ECERS and ECERS-R serve children from age two and half to five. Descriptive and inferential comparisons were also made between baseline assessment and formal assessment to discern whether centers serving children from birth to age two and half improved the quality of their programs (measured by ITERS and ITERS-R). Table 8.3 presents analytical results for centers evaluated with ITERS. A descriptive comparison of means between baseline assessment and formal assessment indicated some changes across all quality indicators. Inferential comparisons revealed that centers demonstrated statistically significant improvement in one quality indicator (activities) and in the overall measure of quality during a period of 13 months from baseline assessment to formal assessment. Improvement in activities was strong (with a large effect size of 0.96). So was the overall improvement (with a large effect size of 0.89). Inferential analysis revealed that changes in other quality indicators were not statistically significant. Repeated measures models were marginal in statistical power in these cases but showed high power in the two cases of statistically significant improvement.

Table 8.3: *Results of Comparison Between Baseline Assessment and Formal Assessment Measures Based on Infant/Toddler Environment Rating Scale (ITERS; Before April 2006)*

	Baseline		Formal				
Measure	*M*	*SD*	*M*	*SD*	*F*	ES	Power
Overall measure	3.09	0.26	3.88	0.32	25.20*	0.89	0.90
Space and furnishing	3.23	1.04	4.03	0.26	1.71	0.36	0.16
Personal care routines	2.02	0.10	2.31	0.39	4.23	0.59	0.30
Language–reasoning	3.76	1.54	4.58	0.57	2.42	0.45	0.20
Activities	3.44	0.32	4.82	0.56	70.17*	0.96	1.00
Interaction	2.96	0.28	3.44	1.18	0.66	0.18	0.09
Program structure	3.24	0.94	3.65	0.78	0.32	0.10	0.07

Note. * $p < 0.05$. *M* = mean. *SD* = standard deviation. ES = effect size.

Compared to ITERS data, ITERS-R data showed even greater improvement across quality indicators. Inferential comparisons in Table 8.4 confirmed that centers evaluated with ITERS-R significantly improved the quality of their programs across all quality indicators during a period of 13 months from baseline assessment to formal assessment. Improvement was great across all quality indicators, with effect size ranging from 0.74 to 0.84. The most improvement occurred in the overall measure of quality (with effect size of 0.84). Individual quality indicators showed highly consistent improvement (with effect size ranging from 0.74 to 0.79). Thus, during a period of 13 months, not only did centers evaluated with ITERS-R experience great improvement in the overall measure of quality, but centers also showed similar amount of improvement across all quality indictors. Repeated measures models showed high statistical power in all cases for detecting differences between baseline assessment and formal assessment.

Table 8.4: *Results of Comparison Between Baseline Assessment and Formal Assessment Measures Based on Revised Infant/Toddler Environment Rating Scale (ITERS-R; April 2006 to Present)*

	Baseline		Formal				
Measure	*M*	*SD*	*M*	*SD*	*F*	ES	Power
Overall measure	3.11	1.00	5.28	0.63	40.64*	0.84	1.00
Space and furnishing	3.17	1.13	5.01	0.75	27.24*	0.77	1.00
Personal care routines	1.89	0.55	3.01	0.93	24.01*	0.75	0.99
Language–reasoning	3.57	1.65	6.46	0.87	23.97*	0.75	0.99
Activities	3.25	0.99	5.80	0.80	29.61*	0.79	1.00
Interaction	3.99	1.42	6.35	0.69	22.63*	0.74	0.99
Program structure	3.33	1.55	6.04	1.03	26.49*	0.77	0.99

Note. * $p < 0.05$. *M* = mean. *SD* = standard deviation. ES = effect size.

In sum, analyses in this section, using ECERS, ECERS-R, ITERS, and ITERS-R, showed that QIS centers significantly improved (at least) some aspects of the quality of their programs during a period of 13 months from baseline assessment to formal assessment. Most improvements were considerable, especially for those centers that entered QIS in recent years (i.e., centers evaluated with ECERS-R and ITERS-R).

Improvement and Year of Entry

An indication from the previous section is that QIS became more and more efficient and effective in improving quality. April of 2005 separated centers with ECERS and ECERS-R. Centers that entered QIS before April of 2005 experienced weak and isolated improvement across quality indicators, whereas centers that entered QIS after April of 2005 experienced strong and comprehensive improvement across quality indicators. April of 2006 separated centers with ITERS and ITERS-R. Centers that entered QIS before April of 2006 experienced isolated (though strong) improvement across quality indicators, whereas centers that entered QIS after April of 2006 experienced comprehensive (and strong) improvement across quality indicators. We investigated these matters further with multiple regression analysis to examine the (exact) year of entry as it related to gain score across quality indicators with control over type of instrument (original or revised).

Table 8.5 indicates that centers entering QIS later were associated with greater improvement in space and furnishing, personal care routines, language reasoning, and activities, even after control over type of instrument (ECERS or ECERS-R). In a measurement scale of 1 to 7, entering QIS one year later would move a center up 0.93 in quality of space and furnishing as well as personal care routines, 1.11 in quality of language reasoning, and 0.91 in quality of activities. Therefore, in a measurement scale of 1 to 7, entering QIS one year later was associated with almost 1 full score increase (more than 1 full score increase in the case of language reasoning). This magnitude represents substantial effects of year of entry. In terms of the overall measure of quality, even after control over type of instrument (ECERS or ECERS-R), entering QIS one year later would move a center up 0.86 (in a measurement scale of 1 to 7). This magnitude is also strong. Overall, we concluded that QIS indeed became more and more efficient and effective in improving quality. Multiple regression models with statistically significant effects accounted for from 20% to 44% of variance in quality indicators. These proportions are sizeable from the perspective of behavioral sciences. This is a good indication of the effectiveness of these multiple regression models.

Table 8.5: *Effects of Year of Entry on Improvement Between Baseline Assessment and Formal Assessment Measures as Measured by ECERS and ECERS-R*

Outcome	Effect	*SE*	R^2
Overall measure	0.86*	0.34	0.42
Space and furnishing	0.93*	0.40	0.27
Personal care routines	0.93*	0.41	0.20
Language–reasoning	1.11*	0.45	0.37
Activities	0.91*	0.43	0.44
Interaction	0.78	0.65	0.18
Program structure	0.34	0.52	0.19

Note. * $p < 0.05$. Effect indicates unstandardized regression coefficient. R^2 measures the proportion of variance in an outcome measure explained by a regression. Year of entry is estimated as the year when a center's baseline measure is established.

Similar to the case of ECERS and ECERS-R, Table 8.6 indicates that centers entering QIS later were associated with larger improvement in personal care routines, interaction, and program structure, even after control over type of instrument (ITERS or ITERS-R). In a measurement scale of 1 to 7, entering QIS one year later would move a center up 0.28 in quality of personal care routines, 0.63 in quality of interaction, and 0.77 in quality of program structure. In addition, entering QIS one year later would move a center up 0.46 in the overall measure of quality, even after control over type of instrument (ITERS or ITERS-R). Although these magnitudes are moderate, entering QIS later did show some moderate advantage, signaling that QIS as a system did have some potential to become more and more efficient and effective in improving quality (over time). Similar to the case of ECERS and ECERS-R, multiple regression models with statistically significant effects accounted for from 31% to 38% of variance in quality indicators. These proportions are sizeable, indicating the effectiveness of these multiple regression models.

Table 8.6: *Effects of Year of Entry on Improvement Between Baseline Assessment and Formal Assessment as Measured by ITERS and ITERS-R*

Outcome	Effect	*SE*	R^2
Overall measure	0.46*	0.18	0.38
Space and furnishing	0.35	0.22	0.19
Personal care routines	0.28*	0.12	0.32
Language–reasoning	0.69	0.32	0.30
Activities	0.39	0.24	0.19
Interaction	0.63*	0.28	0.31
Program structure	0.77*	0.31	0.36

Note. * $p < 0.05$. Effect indicates unstandardized regression coefficient. R^2 measures the proportion of variance in an outcome measure explained by a regression. Year of entry is estimated as the year when a center's baseline measure is established.

In sum, analyses in this section, again using ECERS, ECERS-R, ITERS, and ITERS-R, indicated that centers entering QIS later showed more improvement in the quality of their programs, supporting the notion that QIS became more and more efficient and effective in improving quality (over time). The effects of year of entry were larger for centers serving children from age two and half to five than centers serving children from birth to age two and half.

Discussion

Principal Findings

We aimed to examine improvement in quality indicators of child care and education centers under QIS. We evaluated centers serving children from age two and half to five with ECERS or ECERS-R (depending on when a center entered QIS). We found that centers evaluated with ECERS (before April of 2005) showed small improvement in activities they offered to children during a period of 13 months (from baseline assessment to formal assessment). Centers evaluated with ECERS-R (after April of 2005) showed moderate improvement in space and furnishing, personal care routines, interaction, and program structure as well as large improvement in activities, language reasoning, and overall measure of quality, during a period of 13 months. The most improvement occurred in activities, whereas the smallest improvement occurred in program structure. In addition, centers entering QIS later showed more improvement in space and furnishing, personal care routines, language reasoning, activities, and overall measure of quality. QIS became more and more efficient and effective in improving quality over time. In other words, it took time for QIS to become efficient and effective.

We evaluated centers serving children from birth to age two and half with ITERS or ITERS-R (depending on when a center entered QIS). Centers evaluated with ITERS (before April of 2006) showed great improvement in activities they offered to children and overall measure of quality during a period of 13 months (from baseline assessment to formal assessment). Centers evaluated with ITERS-R (after April of 2006) showed great improvement across all quality indicators (including overall measure of quality) during a period of 13 months. The most improvement occurred in overall measure of quality. Individual quality indicators demonstrated a highly balanced improvement pattern (with a similar amount of much improvement across all quality indictors). Finally, centers entering QIS later showed more improvement in personal care routines, interaction, program structure, and overall measure of quality. QIS became more and more efficient and effective in improving quality over time. Stated differently, it took time for QIS to become efficient and effective.

Given QIS sufficient time (i.e., taking the cases of ECERS-R and ITERS-R), we found that improvement was greater among centers serving children from age two and half to five than centers serving children from birth to age two and half. Overall, our research has demonstrated the effectiveness of QIS on child care and education centers.

Policy Implications

Rohacek et al. (2010) described the current state of research on the issue of quality of early childcare and education.

> While research has told us a lot about key dimensions of quality—for example the role of stable, well-trained staff—and has delineated major barriers to achieving it, we know little about what influences the variation in quality of services, even among programs that face similar challenges. (p. ix)

Having observed so much variation in the quality of early child care and education programs, these researchers asked how "public initiatives [can] help poor-quality programs improve" (p. ix). We noticed that these researchers strongly believed that research has barely begun to address their question. If research along this line is only in its early infancy, we argue that one question goes even before the question of "how" as they asked. That must be the question of "whether." In fact, the literature on educational change, particularly for the purpose of educational quality improvement, is replete with failure, leading to questions being asked as to whether this failure in educational change is *predictable* and whether the problems in education are *intractable* (see Sarason, 1993, 2002). Our first unique contribution to the field addresses this "whether" issue.

Peisner-Feinberg et al. (2000) reported that, of more than 400 centers studied in four states, 8% of infant ones and 24% of preschool ones were of good to excellent quality, compared to 40% of infant ones and 10% of preschool ones rated as poor in quality. QIS is a direct response to such findings. The theory of action or premise of improvement in QIS is to improve "pathways to quality" (see Children's Services Council of Palm Beach County, 2010). These pathways include (percent indicates weight) environment (40%), professional development and staff qualifications (20%), staff to child ratio and group size (10 %), curriculum (15%), and administration and family engagement (15%). The programs we discussed earlier (star rating, early learning coaches, career advisors, the Registry, SEEK scholarship, and WAGE$) are strategies of QIS to improve those pathways. Our data strongly demonstrated that it is possible for this theory or premise to improve the quality of childcare and education centers. Findings of our research clearly indicated that public initiatives like QIS can become efficient and effective in improving the quality of childcare and education centers.

Along with the "how" issue, Rohacek et al. (2010) also alluded to the "what" issue. Because "quality arises from a combination of factors" (p. xiii), what factors, efforts, or programs work together effectively to improve quality of early child care and education? Clough, Bullock, and Ward (2006, p. 1) stated that "there has been too little searching to know what is effective." McNeish, Newman, and Roberts (2002, p. 3) emphasized the need for "the process of systematically locating, critically reviewing and using research findings as the basis for decisions in childcare practice." Our second unique contribution to the field addresses this "what" issue.

The premise of Rohacek et al. (2010) is that center directors are gatekeepers for quality. Nevertheless, these researchers agreed that "Quality Rating and Improvement Systems [QIS] are well positioned to address many needs" they identified in their study (p. xiv). Again, the theory of action in QIS emphasizes pathways to quality. Designed to measure childcare and education practice, both ECERS and ITERS provide useful insights on what works for what quality at the center level because they examine different areas of practice of childcare and education centers. Findings of our research indicate that the QIS approach (premise) of pathways to quality can work, but improvement under such an approach is more difficult in certain areas than others. In other words, we found that quality indicators seldom showed comparable improvement in quality under the QIS approach of pathways to quality. For example, QIS effects on activities appeared early and effect size was largest, while QIS effects on program structure manifested late and effect size was small. We reason that centers have direct control over activities they offer to children, whereas program structure is often mandated by local or state regulations. Systematic initiatives like QIS need to involve both local and state administrations for potential reforms in policy and practice. As a matter of fact, we consider the lack of such involvement (i.e., such involvement fell off the pathways to quality) as one of the major weaknesses of QIS.

Rohacek et al. (2010) considered time as a very important element in educational change for quality improvement, stating that "improving quality is a developmental process" (p. xiii). In educational change, attempting to seek early wins, too often policymakers and administrators jump from one bandwagon to another without giving sufficient time for significant improvement to occur. Our third unique contribution to the field addresses this issue of time as we showed that time (persistence) was the key for comprehensive QIS effects.

Our finding that QIS became more and more efficient and effective in improving quality over time suggests that it takes time for the QIS approach of pathways to quality to produce educational changes (improvements). We have found that all areas of childcare and education practice (space and furnishing, personal care routines, language reasoning, activities, interactions, and program structure) can be significantly improved in a matter of one year as evidenced in results concerning ECERS-R and ITERS-R. This comprehensive improvement happened in the later years of QIS, however. During the first few years of QIS, there was only isolated improvement as evidenced in results concerning ECERS and ITERS. Over time, as QIS gained experiences in developing, coordinating, and synergizing various components of the system, centers that entered QIS late reaped significant improvement in all areas (for the same length of one year). Results of our multiple regression analyses clearly indicate that improvement was accelerating over time. Fortunately, the differences in time in implementing ECERS and ECERS-R (also ITERS and ITERS-R) gave us a rare, unique opportunity to estimate the time it took the QIS approach to improve quality. For centers serving children from two and half to five in age, it is possible to see improvement in activities in one year, whereas improvement in other areas may take as long as three years. For centers serving children from birth to two and half in age, it is possible to see improvement in activities in one year, whereas improvement in other areas may take as long as four years. These periods may indicate the time needed for QIS to develop, coordinate, and synergize various components of the system. These estimates provide some preliminary information on an issue that has yet been addressed in the research literature.

Research Limitations

Several limitations were recognized in the process of this research and evaluation. The major limitation is the lack of a comparable sample of childcare centers that are not part of QIS (i.e., lack of a control group). It is simply impossible to entirely attribute improvement of QIS centers from baseline assessment to formal assessment to participation in QIS. Therefore, the tentative nature of findings of our research needs to be emphasized even though the difficulty in building a control group in large systematic initiatives like QIS is understandable.

Another major limitation is the lack of sufficient data describing characteristics of QIS centers. As a result, it is impossible to purify QIS effects on the basis of center characteristics. Meanwhile, without characteristics of QIS centers, we were unable to identify which center conditions facilitate or hinder improvement in quality.

Although the coincidental encounter with the revision of ECERS and ITERS gave us a rare, unique research opportunity, it did compromise findings of our research. A direct impact is the decrease in sample size for both centers serving children from age two and half to five and centers serving children from birth to age two and half. Multiple regression analysis on the latter involved only 13 centers, a larger sample size will produce more reliable estimates.

Despite the limitations, our research serves as a good starting point in the effort to evaluate large systematic initiatives like QIS. It is important methodologically, as workable strategies are provided to deal with complex situations researchers will surely encounter when they evaluate large systematic initiatives like QIS. It is also important practically, revealing informative findings that will surely promote or maintain reform momentums to improve quality of early childcare and education.

Notes

1. For reasons of space and simplicity, the term, QIS, in the article refers exclusively to the Palm Beach County QIS.
2. The main theory of action in QIS is the concept of pathways to quality. It reflects the belief that efforts of improving those pathways lead to improvement in quality of child care and education centers. Other components facilitate this main theory of action to

take place. All programs (to be discussed next) in QIS are designed to improve those pathways to quality.

3. As a measure of accountability, the county sought external, independent researchers to evaluate the effectiveness of QIS. These researchers conducted case and survey studies, analyzed outcome data on children and sites (provided by the county), and produced research reports (e.g., the present research).
4. Some researchers question the construct of quality that emphasizes definitive and universal criteria that result in certainty and order (e.g., Bloch, 1992; Moss, Dahlberg, & Pence, 2000). Their concern is that quality excludes other perspectives such as complexity, values, diversity, subjectivity, and indeterminacy. They believe that quality is only one way to evaluate early childhood services and their pedagogical work. Alternative approaches to quality include, for example, the concept of meaning making that foregrounds provisionality, multiplicity, and subjectivity.
5. Among the six components of the Palm Beach County QIS, the first component (pathways to quality) forms the empirical basis for data collection and data analysis. Empirical evidence from this component informs other components such as Achievable Standards and Star Ratings. As such, it is the focus of this evaluative research. Both ECERS and ITERS are used to capture data on quality indicators (e.g., space and furnishing, personal care routines) of a childcare center. In other words, both ECERS and ITERS generate data for measuring quality at the center level.

References

Ahn, H.J., & Stifter, C. (2006). Child care teachers' response to children's emotional expression. *Early Education and Development, 17,* 253–270.

American Association of Colleges of Teacher Education. (2004). *The early childhood challenge: Preparing high quality teachers for a changing society* (White paper document # 5369). Retrieved May 14, 2009, from www.ecs.org.

American Educational Research Association. (2005). Early child care and children's development in the primary grades: Follow-up results from the NICHD study of early child care. *American Educational Research Journal, 42,* 537–570.

Bloch, M. N. (1992). Critical science and the relationship between child development research and early education. In S. Kessler & E. B. Swadener (Eds.), *Reconceptualizing early education curriculum: Beginning the dialogue.* New York: Teachers College Press.

Burchinal, M.R., Peisner-Feinberg, E., Pianta, R., & Howes, C. (2002). Development of academic skills from preschool through second grade: Family and classroom predictors of developmental trajectories. *Journal of School Psychology, 40,* 415–436.

Campbell, F.A., Ramey, C.T., Pungello, E., Sparling, J., & Miller-Johnson, S. (2002). Early childhood education: Young adult outcomes from the Abecedarian Project. *Applied Developmental Science, 6,* 42–57.

Children's Services Council of Palm Beach County. (2010). *Quality counts.* Palm Beach, FL: Author.

Clough, R., Bullock, R., & Ward, A. (2006). *What works in residential child care: A review of research evidence and the practical considerations.* London: National Children's Bureau.

Cohen, S.S., & Lord, H. (2005). Implementation of the Child Care and Development Block Grant: A research synthesis. *Nursing Outlook, 53,* 239.e1–239.e6.

Curby, T.W., LoCasale-Crouch, J., Konold, T.R., Pianta, R.C., Howes, C., & Burchinal, M. (2009). The relations of observed Pre-K classroom quality profiles to children's achievement and social competence. *Early Education and Development, 20,* 346–372.

Currie, J. (2001). Early childhood education programs. *Journal of Economic Perspectives, 15,* 213–238.

Dahlberg, G., & Moss, P. (2005). *Ethics and politics in early childhood education.* Oxford: RoutledgeFalmer.

Downer, J.T., Kraft-Sayre, M.E., & Pianta, R.C. (2009). Ongoing, web-mediated professional development focused on teacher-child interactions: Early childhood educators' usage rates and self-reported satisfaction. *Early Education and Development, 20,* 321–-345.

Early, D.M., Bryant, D.M., & Pianta, R.C. (2006). Are teachers' education, major, and credentials related to classroom quality and children's academic gains in pre-kindergarten? *Early Childhood Research Quarterly, 21,* 174–195.

Espinosa, L.M. (2008). *Challenging common myths about young English language learners.* New York: Foundation for Child Development.

Ewen, D. (2005). *The Senate's $6 billion child care provision: A critical, but modest, investment.* Washington, DC: Center for Law and Social Policy.

Huber, L.K. (2003). Knowing children and building relationships with families: A strategy for improving conferences. *Early Childhood Education Journal, 31,* 75–77.

Hynes, K., & Habasevich-Brooks, T. (2008). The ups and downs of child care: Variations in child care quality and exposure across the early years. *Early Childhood Research Quarterly, 23,* 559–574.

Isenberg, J., & Renck-Jalongo, M. (2003). *Major trends and issues in early childhood education: Challenges, controversies, and insights.* New York: Teachers College.

Li-Grining, C. P., & Coley, R.L. (2006). Child care experiences in low-income communities: Developmental quality and maternal views. *Early Childhood Research Quarterly, 21,* 125–141.

Marshall, N.L. (2004). The quality of early child care and children's development. *Current Directions in Psychological Science, 13,* 165–168.

McNeish, D., Newman, T., & Roberts, H. (2002). *What works for children?* Buckingham, UK: Open University Press.

Moss, P., Dahlberg, G., & Pence, A. (2000). Getting beyond the problem with quality. *European Early Childhood Education Research Journal,* 8, 103–115.

National Institute of Child Health and Human Development. (2003). Does quality of child care affect child outcomes at age 4.5? *Developmental Psychology, 39,* 451–469.

Paulsell, D., Nogales, R., & Cohen, J. (2003). *Quality child care for infants and toddlers: Case studies of three community strategies.* Princeton, NJ: Mathematica Policy Research, Inc.

Peisner-Feinberg, E. S., Burchinal, M. R., Clifford, R. M., Culkin, M.L., Howes, C., Kagan, S. L., Yazejian, N., Byler, P., Rustici, J., & Zelazo, J. (2000). *The children of the cost, quality, and outcomes study go to school: Technical report.* Chapel Hill: University of North Carolina at Chapel Hill, Frank Porter Graham Child Development Center.

Pianta, R.C. (2007). Preschool is school, sometimes. *Education Next, 7*(1), 44–49.

Pittard, M., Zaslow, M., Lavelle, B., & Porter, T. (2006). *Investing in quality: A survey of state childcare and development fund initiatives.* Washington, DC: National Association of State Child Care Administrators.

Rohacek, M., Adams, G. C., Kisker, E. E., Danziger, A., Derrick-Mills, T., & Johnson, H. (2010). *Understanding quality in context: Child care centers, communities, markets, and public policy.* Washington, DC: Urban Institute.

Rosenthal, R., & Rosnow, R. L. (1984). *Essentials of behavioral research: Methods and data analysis.* New York: McGraw-Hill.

Rous, B., Hallam, R., Grove, J., Robinson, S., & Machara, M. (2003). *Parent involvement in early care and education programs: A review of the literature.* University of Kentucky, Interdisciplinary Human Development Institute.

Rudd, L.C., Cain, D.W., & Saxon, T.F. (2008). Does improving joint attention in low-quality child care enhance language development? *Early Child Development and Care, 178,* 315–338.

Sachs, J. (2000). Inequities in early care and education: What is America buying? *Journal of Education for Students Placed at Risk, 5,* 383–395.

Saracho, O.N., & Spodek, B. (2007) Early childhood teacher's preparation and the quality of program outcomes. *Early Childhood Development and Care, 1,* 71–91.

Sarason, S.B. (1993). *The predictable failure of educational reform: Can we change course before it's too late.* San Francisco, CA: Jossey-Bass.

Sarason, S.B. (2002). *Educational reform: A self-scrutinizing memoir.* New York: Teachers College.

Shlay, A.B., Tran, H., Weinraub, M., & Harmon, M. (2005). Teasing apart the child care conundrum: A factorial survey analysis of perceptions of child care quality, fair market price and willingness to pay by low-income, African American parents. *Early Childhood Research Quarterly, 20,* 393–416.

Shonkoff, J.P., & Phillips, D.A. (eds.). (2000). *From neurons to neighborhoods: The science of early childhood development.* Washington, DC: National Academy Press.

Takanishi, R., & Kauerz, K. (2008). PK inclusion: Getting serious about a P-16 education system. *Phi Delta Kappa, 89,* 480–87.

Uttley, C.M., & Horm, D.M. (2008). Mentoring in early childhood professional development: Evaluation of the Rhode Island child development specialist apprenticeship program. *Journal of Early Childhood Teacher Education, 29,* 237–252.

Wiltz, N.W., & Klein, E.L. (2001). What do you do in child care? Children's perceptions of high and low quality classrooms. *Early Childhood Research Quarterly, 16,* 209–236.

Zellman, G., & Perlman, M. (2007). *Measuring quality child care.* Santa Monica, CA: RAND.

9

Effects of Quality Improvement System on Childcare Sites' Performance in School Readiness

XIN MA, JIANPING SHEN, XUEJIN LU, KAREN BRANDI, JEFF GOODMAN, AND GRACE WATSON

Formative years, referring to the age from newborn to five years, represent a critical stage of child development. Maria Montessori (1909) viewed the mind of children at this stage as so absorbent that the quality of education can have a long-lasting benefit in their entire lives. The importance of early childhood education has been argued from the perspectives of intellectual, emotional, and social development (see Hawley, 2000; Knudsen, Heckman, Cameron, & Shonkoff, 2006; Shonkoff & Phillips, 2000). The Abecedarian Project was a longitudinal prospective study with early childhood education interventions to infants from low-income, multi-risk families (Campbell, Ramey, Pungello, Sparling, & Miller-Johnson, 2002). Compared with individuals in the preschool control group, those in the preschool intervention group completed significantly more years of education, were significantly more likely to attend a four-year college, and achieved significantly better in intellectual and academic tests as young adults. In fact, the preschool interventions demonstrated long-lasting effects on skills of reading and mathematics all the way into adulthood. Early and Winton (2001) concluded that early childhood education must keep pace with the astounding growth of mental abilities and the high proportion of learning capacities during the formative years of children.

Many efforts have been made to ensure the quality of early childhood education, such as promoting healthy childcare environments, providing formal training and education for childcare providers, and developing effective professional development systems (Pittard, Zaslow, Lavelle, & Porter, 2006). Joining the standards movement in the 1980s, the National Association for the Education of Young Children (NAEYC) took a critical step to establish professional preparation standards for early childhood education programs that are considered important determinants of the quality of early childhood education (see Saracho & Spodek, 2007). To improve quality as a result of these national standards, NAEYC emphasizes both quality rating (as a benchmark to categorize quality of childcare) and quality information (as a way to create awareness of quality). These efforts implemented at the local level result in a systematic approach often referred to as Quality Improvement System (QIS). Oklahoma enacted the first QIS (i.e., Reaching for the Stars) in 1998, and North Carolina launched its QIS (i.e., Star Rated License) in 1999. Since then, 16 more states have implemented QIS and nearly all other states are either developing or considering developing QIS (see Neugebauer, 2009). The Palm Beach County (Florida) QIS (assessed in the present study) was designed and implemented within such a national reform background.

QIS initiatives define levels of childcare quality based on research evidence and support childcare providers with funding and technical assistance to improve childcare quality. There are different programs in a particular QIS, and each program is assessed and given "stars" to inform parents and administrators about the level of childcare quality for a specific provider. In pursuit of quality rating, QIS initiatives adopt and implement multiple assessments designed to make childcare quality measurable, transparent, and understandable. Specifically, childcare providers are assessed on a summary rating system of either 1 to 4 stars or 1 to 5 stars. Quality information interprets the quality rating, usually made public to encourage providers to seek ways to improve quality as well as parents and administrators to make informed choices about which providers to use and support. School readiness is usually among the assessments, considered one of the "ultimate outcomes" of QIS initiatives (see Zellman, Perlman, Le, & Setodji, 2008, p. 5).

Unfortunately, evaluative efforts are lacking regarding the effects of QIS on children's school readiness. Despite the commitment of almost all states to develop and implement QIS, very few studies exist that document the relationship between QIS ratings and child outcomes (Thornburg, Mayfield, Hawks, & Fuger, 2009). "Indeed, there is little information available about these systems, [including] whether children benefit from the improved care they are receiving as their provider receives quality-improvement support" (Zellman et al., 2008, p. 6). Value added longitudinal research designs are even rarer (if not none). As an attempt to fill in some of these gaps, the present study is an advanced application of growth modeling to evaluate the effects of QIS on the growth of childcare site performance in school readiness. Our research came at a historic time. Looking forward to the next decade, stakeholders across this country want prioritized research that generates critical information about the effectiveness of QIS (Tout, Zaslow, Halle, & Forry, 2009).

Review of Literature

In a comprehensive, classic review of the research literature, Doherty (1997) asserted that children's school readiness needs to be understood from five perspectives (five components of school readiness): (a) physical well-being and appropriate motor development, (b) emotional health and a positive approach to new experiences, (c) age-appropriate social knowledge and competence, (d) age-appropriate language skills, and (e) age-appropriate general knowledge and cognitive skills. Thompson (2002) discussed three qualities of school readiness (intellectual, motivational, and socioemotional) as indicators of a child who is prepared to learn. The present study focuses on the assessment of the last two components of Doherty's taxonomy or Thompson's intellectual quality. We define children's school readiness mainly in terms of cognition, referring to children's ability to "perceive, organize, and analyze the information provided by their social and physical environment" (Doherty, 1997, p. 34) so as to build a stronger connection between early childhood and elementary education (see Pianta, Cox, & Snow, 2007).

There can be other definitions of school readiness. In Doherty (1997), each perspective offers an opportunity to define school readiness. We adopted the cognitive definition because we are persuaded that formal schooling in various school core content areas requires certain foundational cognitive skills and children should acquire these skills during their early childhood education (see Pianta et al., 2007). Although academic preparation for formal schooling remains important, some researchers have argued for a paradigm shift (see Carlton & Winsler, 1999; Graue, 1993).

Many characteristics of childcare in the home, childcare facility, and community impact school readiness, according to Thompson (2002) who maintains home as the primary setting for developing school readiness but emphasizes that experiences from childcare facility are critically important, particularly for children who spend considerable time there. The present study focuses on childcare sites (facilities) as they receive QIS support to impact children's school readiness.

What childcare characteristics determine children's school readiness? Zellman et al. (2008) identified high quality programs as the underlining theory of QIS, arguing that these programs improve the everyday caring and learning environment for children, which, in turn, improves learning outcomes (including school readiness) of children. It does appear that high quality childcare is an underlining determinant of school readiness. Ramey and Ramey (2006) argued that high doses of high quality care and extensive support to parents result in the strongest effect sizes for developmental outcomes (including school readiness) of socially disadvantaged children. High quality childcare compensates for the inadequate learning opportunities as well as social and emotional support at home (Heckman, 2006). The NICHD (National Institute of Child Health and Human Development) Study of Early Childcare has been offering excellent opportunities to connect childcare quality and child outcomes (NICHD Early Child Care Research Network, 1994). For example, higher quality in childcare has consistently been linked to higher scores in mathematics, reading, and memory (NICHD Early Child Care Research Network, 2005).

What then are indicators of high quality childcare? According to Zellman et al. (2008), they include rich learning environments, supportive interactions with adults, and scaffolding that encourages exploration. Blair (2002) emphasized education curricula. Shared environment is the largest factor for the core abilities underlining school readiness, accounting also for the predictive association between school readiness and early school achievement (Lemelin et al., 2007). The National Association of Child Care Resource and Referral Agencies (2006) added lower child-staff ratio and better-educated staff as indicators of high quality childcare (see also Zellman & Gates, 2002). Kisker and Maynard (1991) noticed that indicators of high quality childcare can be relative, depending on who is examining childcare. When choosing childcare, parents may pay more attention to personal characteristics of staff (e.g., warmth and brightness) than education and training of staff, child-staff ratio, and curricula.

As QIS emerges as a driving force for high quality childcare, it provides an excellent opportunity to examine the relationship between childcare quality and school readiness. Zellman et al. (2008) evaluated this relationship in the Colorado QIS (i.e., Qualistar Early Learning). They found that childcare quality does improve, but star ratings (quality ratings) have no impact on child outcomes including school readiness. Thornburg et al. (2009) evaluated the same relationship in the Missouri QIS (i.e., Missouri Quality Rating System). With a focus on children in poverty, they reported that both medium and high quality programs improve exposure to and use of new vocabulary among children, thus laying an enhanced foundation for the development of good reading skills. Furthermore, although knowledge of letters and sounds as well as gross motor skills of children improve regardless of program quality, higher quality does correspond to greater improvement in these areas.

In essence, both evaluations failed to demonstrate strong, comprehensive effects of QIS on children's school readiness. Even though the existing literature is limited on the contribution of QIS to children's outcomes (including school readiness), the research literature is in general robust on the link of quality childcare to children's outcomes. The National Institute of Child Health and Human Development (2003) considered childcare quality as a modest but reliable predictor of cognitive development and academic achievement during early childhood. Although gains in academic skills as a result of enrollment in pre-kindergarten (Pre-K) programs are small (Howes et al., 2008), high quality care contributes to positive children's outcomes.

The question that is most pressing in the current field is whether QIS can improve quality and subsequently influence children's outcomes; that is, what is the path to positive children's outcomes? Both Zellman et al. (2008) and Thornburg et al. (2009) attempted to explore this path. The present study joins the above efforts in evaluating the (treatment) effects of QIS on children's school readiness. There are essentially two ways to pursue this goal. A "snapshot" approach focuses on one point in time—often a critical turning point in child development, whereas a growth approach takes a developmental perspective to evaluate change over time. We prefer the growth approach for two reasons. First, this approach is in general appropriate for education, as Willett (1988) argued that "the very notion of learning implies growth and change" (p. 346). Second, this approach may be specifically useful for the present study because early childhood education "changes children's trajectories" (Zellman et al., 2008, p. 2).

We developed a growth model over three years to inquire into the rate of growth in terms of childcare site performance in children's school readiness between QIS and non-QIS sites. We supplemented this growth analysis with traditional cross-sectional comparisons between QIS and non-QIS sites annually in children's school readiness. Our research questions were: (a) Are there any differences in children's school readiness between QIS and non-QIS sites in each year of a three-year period? (b) Is sites' participation in QIS associated with a higher rate of growth in terms of sites' performance in children's school readiness over the three-year period? These two questions were examined for the Palm Beach County (Florida) QIS.

Two things become immediately transparent. First, our analysis is not a panel study in which the same cohort of children is followed over years. Each year, we have a different cohort of children in both QIS and non-QIS sites. Strictly speaking, the present study is a trend analysis (see Ma, 2010). Second, the key unit of analysis is site. The present study is about growth in site performance in children's school readiness rather than growth in child (individual) performance in school readiness. The rationale for this is that QIS is a site-level intervention. QIS works directly with sites rather than children (within sites). It is thus desirable to see whether this site-level intervention can affect a site's school readiness of children as a whole as QIS works with sites to improve quality which may gradually penetrate to children.

Method

Setting

Children's Services Council of Palm Beach County in Florida designed and implemented its QIS as a comprehensive, voluntary, systematic initiative to prepare children for school readiness, with goals to (a) produce positive outcomes for children; (b) provide consumer education for parents; and (c) define, advocate for, and obtain the resources necessary to encourage, support, and promote quality early care and education. There are six components: (a) six pathways to quality (emphasizing environment, professional development, staff to child ratio, management, parental involvement, curriculum, and child development screening), (b) achievable standards (developing a fair system for rating a childcare site and developing a roadmap for achieving high quality), (c) star ratings (indicating to what extent a childcare site has met quality criteria), (d) reliable assessments (ensuring a fair, consistent, and accurate assessment process for each childcare site by adopting nationally recognized, research based, assessment tools to evaluate the quality of childcare sites), (e) quality improvement supports (providing financial and technical supports to childcare sites and their staff), and (f) consumer education opportunities (informing parents and staff of a childcare site's commitment to quality).

Licensed childcare sites, school based childcare sites, and family childcare homes that hold a rate agreement with the county to accept children receiving subsidies were invited to participate in QIS, with 150 out of about 600 sites volunteering. QIS programs included: (a) star rating (assessing outcomes of sites for quality improvement), (b) early learning coaches (visiting sites to provide on-site technical assistance for overall quality improvement), (c) career advisors (pairing early childhood practitioners with advisors to provide career guidance), (d) workshops and conferences (approved or offered by Palm Beach Community College for practitioners to earn credits toward certificate and degree), (e) SEEK scholarship (allocating funds for practitioners to pursue continuing education), and (f)

WAGE$ (providing financial support to retain practitioners in the profession). QIS sites were required to take part in star rating, early learning coaches, career advisors, and workshops (for certification). SEEK (scholarship) is available (first come, first served) to attend conferences. Almost all practitioners obtained WAGE$ (as salary supplement).

With no funding from the state, Palm Beach County initiated a property tax to fund QIS. Started in 2002, sites received funding and support at a higher level during the first year (the intensive phase) and continued to receive services during the maintenance phase as long as they chose to stay in QIS (95% of sites did stay for at least one year in the maintenance phase). As a measure of accountability, external, independent researchers were used to evaluate the effectiveness of QIS. These researchers conducted case and survey studies, and they analyzed outcome data on children and sites.

Sample

Children's Services Council provided 87 QIS sites that as a group were comparable to 88 non-QIS sites (as a group) in terms of children's socioeconomic and racial-ethnic background. Among the 87 QIS sites, as long as a site had school readiness measures in one year from 2006 to 2008, it was included in the present study, resulting in 18 QIS sites. The same procedure resulted in 28 non-QIS sites. These sites were either licensed childcare ones or school-based childcare ones. The Appendix presents a comparison of site characteristics. There were not statistically significant differences in site characteristics between QIS and non-QIS sites. The only exception was the type of program where all QIS sites were school-year program, compared with 68 percent of non-QIS sites. This variable was statistically controlled in the growth model analysis. We made a comparison with the Missouri QIS with 38 sites from Kansas City, St. Joseph, and Columbia (see Thornburg et al., 2009). Our sample therefore involved a larger number of sites from a smaller region.

Outcome Measures

Five school readiness measures were employed in the present study. School Readiness Rate was measured as score point (0 to 300). Early Childhood Observation System (ECHOS) was measured as a percent of children ready for school in each childcare site. Letter Naming Fluency (LNF) was adopted from Dynamic Indicators of Basic Early Literacy Skills (DIBELS) and was measured as a percent of children ready for school in each childcare site. Initial Sound Fluency (ISF) was adopted also from DIBELS and was measured as a percent of children ready for school in each childcare site. Low Performing Provider (LPP) was measured as whether or not a site was designated as a low performing provider.

Developed by Harcourt Assessment, ECHOS is an observation system for grades K-2 that combines technology with ongoing observation in the classroom to help practitioners monitor the progress of learning among children and guide classroom instruction. Harcourt Assessment justifies validity for ECHOS on the basis of alignment to the guidelines and standards of many national organizations such as NAEYC and the National Research Council Committee on the Prevention of Reading Difficulties in Young Children. Reliability information is not available from Harcourt Assessment. DIBELS measures acquisition of early literacy skills for grades K-6 (see Kaminski, Cummings, Powell-Smith, & Good, 2008).

Specifically, 19 items were adopted from ECHOS to align with key child development domains: (a) approaches to learning (1 item), (b) social and emotional (2 items), (c) language and communication (1 item), (d) emergent literacy (4 items), (e) cognitive development and general knowledge (9 items), and (f) motor development (2 items). A kindergarten teacher observes a child in his or her natural environment on these skills and rates the child's skill development. LNF consists of a page of random letters in upper and lower cases. A child names as many letters as possible in one minute. For ISF, the examiner reads four sets of four words (for a total of 16 items) and asks which word begins with a particular sound. In one minute, a child points to as many pictures as possible representing the words to indicate the correct answers. Scores for both LNF and ISF are reported as number of correct responses per minute.

A percentage of children ready for school on each of the three measures (ECHOS, LNF, and ISF) is calculated by dividing the number of children who score at or above the level for school readiness on each measure by the number of children screened on each measure. The sum of the three percentages becomes School Readiness Rate for each childcare site, which ranges from 0 to 300. Sites at the bottom 15 percent of School Readiness Rate are designated as LPP by Florida Department of Education.

Although ECHOS, LNF, and ISF were independent measures, School Readiness Rate and LPP were derived either directly or indirectly from them for different purposes with School Readiness Rate focusing on average performance whereas LPP focusing on low performance. Florida Department of Education designates sites at the bottom 15 percent of School Readiness Rate as LPP for all sites in the state. Therefore, it is possible for both QIS and non-QIS sites to have a percent larger than 15 as LPP when grouped into their own category.

Statistical Analysis

We first performed traditional cross-sectional comparisons between QIS and non-QIS sites in terms of the five measures of children's school readiness separately for each of the three years (2006, 2007, and 2008). Statistical analysis took the form of multiple regression analysis with school readiness as the dependent variable and participation in QIS (i.e., QIS membership) as the key independent variable. The research community realizes that improvement in academic measures tends to be slow (requiring sufficient time to observe improvement). Especially, when an intervention does not work directly with children, improvement in their academic measures may take considerable time to occur. This is the case of QIS where the penetration of "benefits" from practitioners to children was expected to be slow and gradual. This is why QIS started to collect school readiness data a few years after it began in 2002. This situation contributed to the relatively small number of QIS sites in the present study (see discussion on sample).

The growth model approach was then adopted to examine changes over time in school readiness measures (from 2006 to 2008). Statistical analysis of changes in these school readiness measures took the form of hierarchical linear models (HLM) (see Raudenbush & Bryk, 2002). In the present study, there were longitudinal data on school readiness measures at the site level from 2006 to 2008 (repeated measures on each school readiness measure). HLM took into account this data hierarchy with repeated measures nested within childcare sites. Each school readiness measure was examined in a separate HLM growth model analysis.

We performed HLM growth model analyses based on repeated measures on school readiness at the site level. Of course, site-level school readiness measures came from individual children's scores on school readiness measures. An ideal HLM growth model would be a three-level model with repeated measures nested within children nested within sites. However, we could not build HLM from the child level because children were assessed within 30 days after they entered kindergarten. In other words, we did not have a panel design that follows the same cohort of children over time because children attending kindergarten changed every year (within each year very few children transferred in or out nevertheless). Therefore, the longitudinal perspective of the data could be capitalized not at the child level but at the site level. QIS had data on site-level school readiness measures as we discussed earlier.

The key estimate from a HLM growth model analysis is the rate of growth that describes a trajectory of change over time in an outcome measure. In the present study, the rate of growth depicted a linear change (positive or negative or zero meaning no change) of childcare sites over three years in each of the five school readiness measures. The rate of growth in school readiness measures would then be compared between QIS and non-QIS sites. This comparative function was achieved by creating a dummy variable representing these two specific groups of sites.

Site characteristics were used as control variables to adjust for QIS effects in both cross-sectional (multiple regression) and longitudinal (growth model) analyses. These variables included (a) percent of male children, (b) percent of White children, (c) percent of children with disability, (d) percent of children with limited English proficiency, (e) percent of children eligible for free or reduced-price lunch, (f) number of children served, (g) school-year program (vs. summer program) (a dummy variable), (h) private site (vs. public site) (a dummy variable), and (i) faith-based site (vs. non-faith-based site) (a dummy variable). These variables provided adequate control over contextual characteristics of sites to adjust the effects of QIS. Controlling for contextual characteristics of an educational organization is always important when estimating effects at the organization level (Teddlie & Reynolds, 2000).

Other site-related variables such as education and salary of practitioners are not available. In fact, the use of a large number of variables descriptive of site characteristics would have created a statistical concern given our rather small sample of sites. There were categories of Whites, Blacks, Hispanics, and Asians in the measure of ethnicity. We used only the percentage of Whites to reduce the number of site variables (also to avoid small percentages of minority groups).

Results

Table 9.1 presents descriptive statistics on the five school readiness measures between QIS and non-QIS sites over the three years (2006, 2007, and 2008). Comparisons of means between QIS and non-QIS sites indicated a trend of convergence across years. Most evident of this trend was ECHOS. Specifically, in 2006, the difference in ECHOS between QIS and non-QIS sites was almost 4 percentage points. In 2007, the difference became less than 1 percentage point. In 2008, there was hardly any difference in ECHOS between QIS and non-QIS sites.

Table 9.1: *Descriptive Statistics of School Readiness Measures Between QIS and Non-QIS Sites, by Year*

	2006		2007		2008	
	Mean	SD	Mean	SD	Mean	SD
School Readiness Rate						
QIS sites	219.02	40.89	235.40	40.32	234.97	36.46
Non-QIS sites	239.38	31.59	232.38	40.21	232.90	36.66
ECHOS						
QIS sites	84.31	14.24	91.43	10.53	89.41	10.03
Non-QIS sites	87.50	12.19	90.55	12.13	89.70	8.26
LNF						
QIS sites	72.57	19.22	79.00	18.55	81.72	15.26
Non-QIS sites	82.35	15.54	78.71	19.34	82.29	14.64
ISF						
QIS sites	62.14	19.25	64.79	19.22	63.84	18.38
Non-QIS sites	69.65	13.77	63.12	15.71	60.92	20.73
LPP						
QIS sites	26.53	44.61	14.52	35.51	22.95	42.40
Non-QIS sites	15.19	36.12	25.76	44.06	28.57	45.54

Note. Means for School Readiness Rate are score points. Means for ECHOS, LNF, and ISF are percentages of children who have met the developmental threshold for each particular measure. Means for LPP are percentages of sites designated as such.

In addition, some comparisons indicated a trend of QIS sites gaining some advantages over non-QIS sites as time progressed. Most evident of this trend were ISF and LPP. For example, in 2006, the difference in ISF between QIS and non-QIS sites was about 8 percentage points in favor of non-QIS sites. In 2007, the difference was about 2 percentage points in favor of QIS sites. In 2008, the advantage of QIS sites in ISF (over non-QIS sites) increased to about 3 percentage points.

Results of cross-sectional analysis by year are presented in Table 9.2. Differences between QIS and non-QIS sites were tested for statistical significance in each of the five school readiness measures with control for site characteristics across the three years. Overall, for each of the five school readiness measures, QIS sites were not different statistically from non-QIS sites in each of the three years. This conclusion appears to indicate a comprehensive lack of QIS effects over the three years. Nevertheless, cross-sectional analysis by year cannot be employed to show any trend across years. We therefore adopted a growth model approach for this purpose. As a matter of fact, results of this growth model approach effectively illustrate a flaw with cross-sectional analysis by year that can miss out important differences in trend due to treatment or intervention.

Table 9.2: *Comparison in School Readiness Measures between QIS and Non-QIS Sites with Control for Site Characteristics*

	2006		2007		2008	
	Effect	SE	Effect	SE	Effect	SE
Readiness Rate	5.55	11.92	1.65	5.90	-1.84	5.49
ECHOS	-3.11	1.92	0.41	1.32	0.13	2.83
LNF	-7.12	6.33	-2.64	2.54	1.96	2.77
ISF	9.48	5.62	3.01	2.90	1.28	3.81
LPP	0.44	0.63	-1.27	0.84	-0.84	0.56

Note. * $p < 0.05$. Effect represents unstandardized regression coefficient. SE = standard error.

The HLM growth model that we employed estimated a linear trajectory for QIS and non-QIS sites. Although descriptive statistics in Table 9.1 might not suggest a good linear trend, with only 3 time points it is the best statistical practice to fit a linear line. A higher power (e.g., quadratic or cubic) fit typically requires more time points. As reported earlier, each of the five school readiness measures was examined separately in a HLM growth model analysis. Three of the five measures (School Readiness Rate, ECHOS, and LNF) did not show any QIS effects either without or with statistical control of childcare site characteristics. This means that QIS sites grew at the same rate as non-QIS sites in each of these three school readiness measures over the three years. Because of this situation, we reported analytical results mainly in terms of ISF and LPP, the two school readiness measures that showed statistically significant QIS effects on the rate of growth after adjustment over site characteristics.

Tables 9.3 and 9.4 present the QIS effects on the rate of growth over the three years (from 2006 to 2008) in ISF and LPP. Estimates reported in each table represent the results from a parsimonious growth model that contains statistically significant childcare site characteristics only. ISF is a continuous outcome (dependent variable), requiring a regular HLM growth model (Table 9.3). LPP is a dichotomous outcome, requiring a logistic HLM growth model (Table 9.4).

Table 9.3: *QIS Effects on Rate of Growth in Initial Sound Fluency with Control for Site Characteristics*

	Effect	SE
Initial (2006) status		
QIS sites (vs. non-QIS sites)	-4.65	(3.55)
Percent of children eligible for free or reduced-price lunch	0.24*	(0.07)
Rate of growth (from 2006 to 2008)		
QIS sites (vs. non-QIS sites)	5.80*	(2.23)

Note. * $p < 0.05$. Effect represents unstandardized coefficient. SE = standard error.

Table 9.4: *QIS Effects on Rate of Growth in Probability of Becoming a Low Performing Provider with Control for Site Characteristics*

	Effect	SE	Exp
Initial (2006) status			
QIS sites (vs. non-QIS sites)	1.45*	(0.64)	4.25
Percent of children eligible for free or reduced-price lunch	-0.10*	(0.02)	[1.11]
School-year program (vs. summer program)	-1.81*	(0.68)	[6.25]
Rate of growth (from 2006 to 2008)			
QIS sites (vs. non-QIS sites)	-0.98*	(0.35)	[2.63]

Note. * $p < 0.05$. Effect represents unstandardized coefficient. SE = standard error. Exp = *e* raised to the power of the effect. For consistency of interpretation, Exp of the negative effect is reported as its reciprocal in parenthesis.

The QIS effects were examined in terms of both initial status and rate of growth in ISF (Table 9.3). Initial status represents site performance in ISF in 2006 when growth began. There were not statistically significant QIS effects on initial (2006) status, after controlling for childcare site characteristics (percent of children eligible for free or reduced-price lunch was statistically significant). Rate of growth in ISF (from 2006 to 2008) was the focus of Table 9.3. QIS sites grew statistically significantly faster than non-QIS sites in ISF (no site characteristics were statistically significant). Specifically, the rate of growth of QIS sites was nearly 6 percentage points higher than that of non-QIS sites. Relating this conclusion with Table 9.1, we can see that non-QIS sites experienced a consistent decline in ISF, whereas QIS sites demonstrated an upward trend in ISF (see Table 9.1). The magnitude of the QIS effects (nearly 6 percentage points) is sizeable. Its corresponding effect size is

0.33. Rosenthal and Rosnow (1984) classifies effect sizes more than 0.50 as large, between 0.30 and 0.50 as moderate, and less than 0.30 as small. Therefore, compared with non-QIS sites, QIS sites made good progress in raising site performance in ISF over the course of the three years (from 2006 to 2008).

Meanwhile, Table 9.4 indicates that QIS sites were statistically more likely to become LPP than non-QIS sites in 2006 (initial status), after controlling for child-care site characteristics (percent of children eligible for free or reduced-price lunch and school-year program was statistically significant). With a focus on rate of growth (from 2006 to 2008), QIS sites grew statistically significantly slower than non-QIS sites in terms of the probability of becoming LPP (no site characteristics were statistically significant). In other words, over those three years, QIS sites became increasingly unlikely to become LPP, compared with non-QIS sites. Again, relating this conclusion to Table 9.1, we can see that over those three years a consistently increasing percentage of non-QIS sites became LPP, whereas the percentage of QIS sites that became LPP demonstrated an overall declining trend over those three years. Quantitatively, the probability of becoming LPP grew nearly 3 times as fast for non-QIS sites than QIS sites over the course of the three years. Such a magnitude of the QIS effects is considerable, indicating that QIS sites made considerably faster departures from becoming LPP than non-QIS sites (from 2006 to 2008).

In sum, although there was no evidence of comprehensive QIS effects across measures of children's school readiness, we discovered a unique phenomenon that we refer to as "local" QIS effects. We define local as specific aspects, sub-domains, or individual components of school readiness measures. In terms of the rate of growth (from 2006 to 2008), QIS sites "scored" over non-QIS sites in two of the five school readiness measures (ISF and LPP). Meanwhile, QIS sites did not fall behind non-QIS sites in terms of the rate of growth in the remaining three measures (School Readiness Rate, ECHOS, and LNF).

Discussion

Summary of Principal Findings

Our research question was whether QIS sites were able to show greater growth in school readiness than non-QIS sites. We adopted a growth model approach to investigate the rate of growth between QIS and non-QIS sites in five measures of children's school readiness over a period of three years (from 2006 to 2008). These measures included School Readiness Rate, ECHOS, LNF, ISF, and LPP.

We found that QIS sites grew significantly faster than non-QIS sites in ISF (from 2006 to 2008). The rate of growth of QIS sites was nearly 6 percentage points higher than that of non-QIS sites, over the course of three years. We also found that non-QIS sites grew significantly faster than QIS sites in terms of the probability of becoming LPP. The probability of becoming LPP grew nearly 3 times as fast for non-QIS sites than for QIS sites, over the course of three years. On the other hand, QIS sites grew at the same rate as non-QIS sites in School Readiness Rate, ECHOS, and LNF, over the course of three years.

Unique Aspect of QIS Effects

Digesting analytical results from the growth models, we recognized a unique aspect of QIS effects. It appears that QIS was not able to uniformly improve school readiness measures across QIS sites. That is, among QIS sites, there was not any comprehensive improvement as a result of participation in QIS. The lack of QIS effects in School Readiness Rate, ECHOS, and LNF speaks to this conclusion. However, QIS appears effective in helping improve the quality of those QIS sites that were ranked at the bottom. The significant QIS effects on LPP speaks to this conclusion. Two scenarios are possible. First, participation in QIS helped move some LPP sites out of that category. Second, although some QIS sites were heading toward LPP, participation in QIS helped prevent these QIS sites from really becoming LPP.

Again, we consider this unique phenomenon "local" QIS effects. Interestingly, these local QIS effects are not limited to LPP. The other significant QIS effects indicate that QIS sites grew faster in ISF than non-QIS sites. On the other hand, QIS sites grew at the same rate as non-QIS sites in School Readiness Rate. We want to emphasize the fact that School Readiness Rate is calculated as the sum of the percentages from ECHOS, LNF, and ISF. The lack of QIS effects on School Readiness Rate is therefore an indicator that QIS appears to be unable to uniformly improve QIS sites across school readiness measures. Locally, however, there was a significantly faster rate of growth in ISF in favor of QIS sites. Participation in QIS helped excel QIS sites in ISF, over non-QIS sites.

These local QIS effects are very encouraging news, given that change aimed at children is often a long and difficult process, especially when change is attempted at the system level (e.g., at the site level rather than at the child level). Although QIS affects sites and teachers directly, it affects children indirectly. There is some evidence from the present analysis that QIS effects have begun to permeate down to children, even though QIS effects tend to be local at this stage. This represents our hope that treatments or interventions such as QIS may be able to make positive, cumulative effects on children, when given sufficient time.

Overall, we are confident in offering two conclusions on QIS effects. The first conclusion is that participation in QIS appears to be able to lift QIS sites out of the LPP category or prevent QIS sites from falling into the LPP category (i.e., improving worst sites more than anything else). The second conclusion is that QIS effects appear to be able to "locally" permeate down to children (i.e., improving very specific aspects of children's school readiness).

Revisit of Research Literature

We want to emphasize that the unique QIS effects that we found in the present analysis stand out in the research literature on QIS. For the Colorado QIS, Zellman et al. (2008) claimed that star ratings have no impact on children's school readiness. For the Missouri QIS, Thornburg et al. (2009) claimed that children gain in school readiness measures independently of participation in QIS. Therefore, both studies have revealed a total lack of QIS effects on children's school readiness. However, for the Florida QIS (developed and implemented by the Children's Services Council of Palm Beach County), the results suggest that there are significant local QIS effects on children's school readiness.

Of course, these three evaluation studies cannot be compared directly because of a lack of uniformity in measurement instruments (on school readiness). To some extent, however, this lack of uniformity is a positive thing in that it reinforces our unique (local) QIS effects. A reasonable summary of the existing research evaluations on QIS effects would state that QIS does appear to have some very specific effects on children's school readiness that, we hypothesize, must be related to the emphasis and operation of QIS as well as the intensity and duration of engagement of childcare sites in QIS. Such a position makes the two conclusions that we presented in the previous section even more outstanding in the research literature.

Methodological Consideration

Statistically significant QIS effects from the HLM growth models, in contrast to the comprehensive lack of QIS effects from cross-sectional analyses by year, speak to an important methodological issue. Cross-sectional analysis by year is not reliable for estimating trends due to treatment or intervention. Although it is a common practice for researchers to perform cross-sectional analysis by year as a means to address the issue of trend or change in the absence of data from panel design (that follows the same cohort of children over a period of time), the results are subject to the uncertainties of condition changes among QIS and non-QIS sites over time. This situation is far more serious in cross-sectional design than panel design, because children in the sites are different every year in cross-sectional design.

Specifically, panel design generates "true" longitudinal data that logically call for a growth model approach for data analysis. On the other hand, when each year has a different cohort of children, the most straightforward strategy is to synthesize analytical results year by year (as a way to detect trend or change). We have demonstrated in Tables 9.2 to 9.4 that such a strategy can miss out important trends or changes due to treatment or intervention. We believe that a more appropriate strategy is to treat data of different cohorts year by year as "quasi longitudinal" so that a growth model approach is logically called for. The HLM framework has the capacity to accommodate quasi-longitudinal data. In the absence of panel design, this "multivariate" approach that examines years together, we believe, is more appropriate than the "univariate" approach that examines years separately.

Future Research

We are intrigued by the unique QIS effects as we reported above. Nevertheless, data we have at hand do not permit us to look into the mechanism of those unique QIS effects. Why was QIS able to make the worst childcare sites better rather than the best childcare sites even better? One way to understand this issue is to quantify the engagement level of sites. The intensity of participation in QIS may explain the unique QIS effects. This approach requires administrative data that sufficiently document the participation of each QIS site and evaluative data that indicate changes in the caring and learning environment as a result of participation in QIS from the perspective of both site directors and site teachers.

We are also intrigued by the finding that QIS was able to promote a greater rate of growth in ISF only. Why not LNF? One way to understand this phenomenon is to find out whether QIS somehow prepared teachers to work with children more effectively on ISF than LNF. For example, future studies may engage in an alignment study between QIS components (including professional development) and domains of both ISF and LNF. This alignment approach will provide sufficient insight into the impact pattern of QIS in terms of children's school readiness. For example, children's performance in ISF may benefit greatly if some components of QIS (e.g., special trainings) result in intensive verbal interactions between teachers and children.

We admit that there are many standardized measures of children's school readiness. The Florida QIS employed ECHOS and DIBELS (of which LNF and

ISF are parts). Further QIS studies may consider other measures of school readiness such as Early Childhood Classroom Observation Measure (ECCOM), Assessment of Practice in Early Elementary Classrooms (APEEC), and Early Language and Literacy Classroom Observation (ELLCO) (see Maxwell, McWilliam, Hemmeter, Ault, & Schuster, 2001; Smith & Dickinson, 2002; Stipek & Byler, 2004). These measures have some advantages over ECHOS because they are scored by objective, trained professionals rather than by site practitioners. In addition, the use of diverse school readiness measures within and across QIS studies creates excellent opportunities to identify not only sensitive outcome measures but also elements (domains) of early child development that can be effectively influenced by systematic initiatives such as QIS.

References

Blair, C. (2002). School readiness: Integrating cognition and emotion in a neurobiological conceptualization of children's functioning at school entry. *American Psychologist, 57,* 111–127.

Campbell, F. A., Ramey, C. T., Pungello, E., Sparling, J., & Miller-Johnson, S. (2002). Early childhood education: Young adult outcomes from the Abecedarian Project. *Applied Developmental Science, 6,* 42–57.

Carlton, M. P., & Winsler, A. (1999). School readiness: The need for a paradigm shift. *School Psychology Review, 28,* 338–352.

Doherty, G. (1997). *Zero to six: The basics for school readiness.* Ottawa: Human Resources Development Canada.

Early, D. E., & Winton, P. J. (2001). Preparing the workforce: Early childhood teacher preparation at 2- and 4-year institutions of higher education. *Early Childhood Research Quarterly, 16,* 285–306.

Graue, M. E. (1993). *Ready for what: Constructing meanings of readiness for kindergarten.* Albany: State University of New York Press.

Hawley, T. (2000). *Starting smart: How early experiences affect brain development* (2nd ed.). Chicago, IL: Ounce of Prevention Fund.

Heckman, J. J. (2006). A broader view of what education policy should be. In N. F. Watt, C. Ayoub, R. H. Bradley, J. E. Puma, & W. A. LeBouef (eds.), *The crisis in youth mental health: Critical issues and effective programs (Vol. 4): Early intervention programs and policies* (pp. 3–26). Westport, CT: Praeger.

Howes, C., Burchinal, M., Pianta, R., Bryant, D., Early, D., Clifford, R., & Barbarin, O. (2008). Ready to learn? Children's pre-academic achievement in pre-kindergarten programs. *Early Childhood Research Quarterly, 23,* 27–50.

Kaminski, R., Cummings, K. D., Powell-Smith, K. A., & Good, R. H. III (2008). Best practices in using Dynamic Indicators of Basic Early Literacy Skills for formative assessment and evaluation. In A. Thomas & J. Grimes (eds.) *Best practices in school psychology* (Vol. 4) (pp. 1181–1204). Bethesda, MD: National Association of School Psychologists.

Kisker, E. E., & Maynard, R. (1991). Quality, cost, and parental choice of child care. In D. M. Blau (ed.), *The economics of child care* (pp. 127–143). New York: Russell Sage Foundation.

Knudsen, E. I., Heckman, J. J., Cameron, J. L., & Shonkoff, J. (2006). Economic, neurobiological, and behavioral perspectives on building America's future workforce. *Proceedings of the National Academy of Sciences, 103,* 10155–10162.

Lemelin, J., Boivin, M., Forget-Dubois, N., Dionne, G., Séguin, J. R., Brendgen, M., Vitaro, F., Tremblay, R. E., & Pérusse, D. (2007). The genetic-environmental etiology of cognitive school readiness and later academic achievement in early childhood. *Child Development, 78,* 1855–1869.

Ma, X. (2010). Longitudinal evaluation designs. In P. Peterson, E. Baker, & B. McGaw (eds.), *International Encyclopedia of Education* (Vol. 3) (pp. 757–764). Oxford: Elsevier.

Maxwell, K. L., McWilliam, R. A., Hemmeter, M. L., Ault, M. J., & Schuster, J. W. (2001). Predictors of developmentally appropriate practices in kindergarten through third grade. *Early Childhood Research Quarterly, 16,* 431–452.

Montessori, M. (1909). *The Montessori method.* New York: Frederick A. Stokes.

National Association of Child Care Resource and Referral Agencies. (2006). *Breaking the piggy bank: Parents and the high price of child care.* Arlington, VA: Author.

National Institute of Child Health and Human Development. (2003). Does quality of child care affect child outcomes at age 4-1/2? *Developmental Psychology, 39,* 451–469.

Neugebauer, R. (2009). Quality rating and improvement systems: A strategic movement for defining quality. *Exchange, 188,* 66–68.

NICHD Early Child Care Research Network. (1994). Child care and child development: The NICHD Study of Early Child Care. In S. L. Friedman & H. C. Haywood (eds.), *Developmental follow-up: Concepts, domains, and methods* (pp. 377–396). New York: Academic Press.

NICHD Early Child Care Research Network. (2005). Early child care and children's development in the primary grades: Follow-up results from the NICHD Study of Early Child Care. *American Educational Research Journal, 42,* 537–570.

Pianta, R. C., Cox, M. J., & Snow, K. L. (eds.) (2007). *School readiness and the transition to kindergarten in the era of accountability.* Baltimore, MD: Brookes.

Pittard, M., Zaslow, M., Lavelle, B., & Porter, T. (2006). *Investing in quality: A survey of state childcare and development fund initiatives.* Washington, DC: National Association of State Child Care Administrators.

Ramey, C. T., & Ramey, S. L. (2006). Early learning and school readiness: Can early intervention make a difference? In N. F. Watt, C. Ayoub, R. H. Bradley, J. E. Puma, & W. A. LeBouef (eds.), *The crisis in youth mental health: Critical issues and effective programs* (Vol. 4): *Early intervention programs and policies* (pp. 291–318). Westport, CT: Praeger.

Raudenbush, S. W., & Bryk, A. S. (2002). *Hierarchical linear models* (2nd ed.). Newbury Park, CA: Sage.

Rosenthal, R., & Rosnow, R. L. (1984). *Essentials of behavioral research: Methods and data analysis.* New York: McGraw-Hill.

Saracho, O. N., & Spodek, B. (2007). Early childhood teacher's preparation and the quality of program outcomes. *Early Childhood Development and Care, 1,* 71–91.

Shonkoff, J. P., & Phillips, D. (2000). *From neurons to neighborhoods: The science of early child development.* Washington, DC: National Academy Press.

Smith, M. W., & Dickinson, D. K. (2002). *User's guide to the Early Language and Literacy Classroom Observation toolkit.* Baltimore, MD: Brookes Publishing.

Stipek, D., & Byler, P. (2004). The early childhood classroom observation measure. *Early Childhood Research Quarterly, 19,* 375–397.

Teddlie, C., & Reynolds, D. (eds.). (2000). *The international handbook of school effectiveness research.* London: Falmer.

Thompson, R. A. (2002). The roots of school readiness in social and emotional development. In Ewing Marion Kauffman Foundation (ed.), *Set for success: Building a strong foundation for school readiness based on the social-emotional development of young children* (pp. 8–29). Kansas City, MO: Author.

Thornburg, K. R., Mayfield, W. A., Hawks, J. S., & Fuger, K. L. (2009). *The Missouri Quality Rating System school readiness study.* Columbia, MO: Center for Family Policy & Research.

Tout, K., Zaslow, M., Halle, T., & Forry, N. (2009). *Issues for the next decade of quality rating and improvement systems.* Washington, DC: U.S. Department of Health and Human Services.

Willett, J. B. (1988). Questions and answers in the measurement of change. In E. Z. Rothkopf (ed.), *Review of research in education* (pp. 345–422). Washington, DC: American Educational Research Association.

Zellman, G. L., & Gates, S. M. (2002). *Examining the cost of military child care.* Santa Monica, CA: RAND.

Zellman, G. L., Perlman, M., Le, V., & Setodji, C. M. (2008). *Assessing the validity of the Qualistar early learning quality rating and improvement system as a tool for improving child-care quality.* Santa Monica, CA: RAND.

Appendix: *Site Characteristics between QIS Sites and Non-QIS Sites*

	QIS sites		Non-QIS sites	
	Mean	SD	Mean	SD
Percent of male children	0.35	0.12	0.36	0.12
Percent of White children	0.40	0.18	0.41	0.13
Percent of children with disability	0.69	0.17	0.67	0.20
Percent of children with limited English proficiency	0.59	0.17	0.58	0.18
Percent of children eligible for free or reduced-price lunch	0.40	0.22	0.45	0.20
Percent of school-year program (vs. summer program)	**1.00**	0.00	**0.68**	0.48
Percent of private sites (vs. public sites)	0.83	0.38	0.68	0.48
Percent of faith-based sites (vs. non-faith-based sites)	0.17	0.38	0.07	0.26

Note. Means in bold face are statistically significantly different (at the alpha level of 0.05). A decimal represents a percent (e.g., 0.35 = 35 percent). Number of children served is 44 (SD = 25) for QIS sites and 35 (SD = 14) for non-QIS sites (means do not differ statistically significantly).

Section IV. Summary

10

Important Learnings from Evaluating the Quality Improvement System in Palm Beach County

JIANPING SHEN, XIN MA, XUEJIN LU, AND HUILAN Y. KRENN

Quality Improvement System (QIS) as a Staff Development Program

The importance of early childhood education is well documented (Belfield, 2004; Espinosa, 2008; Nelson, 2006; Shlay, Tran, Weinraub, & Harmon, 2005; Shonkoff & Phillips, 2000; Takanishi & Kauerz, 2008). Guided by a general research consensus in the early childhood education literature that "specific conditions are essential at the system level to ensure that high quality at the program level is the norm rather than the exception" (Friendly et al., 2006, p. 15), many state childcare agencies have chosen to, among others, provide informal and formal education and strengthen staff development (Pittard, Zaslow, Lavelle, & Porter, 2006). Improving the quality of early childhood educators and childcare sites becomes the focus of the Quality Improvement System movement (Isenberg & Renck-Jalongo, 2003; Zellman, Perlman, Le & Setodji, 2008).

The Quality Improvement System (QIS), designed and implemented at Palm Beach County, Florida, is such a system-level initiative. It is a comprehensive, voluntary, early care and education improvement system that aims to improve the quality of childcare from birth to age 5. QIS seeks to prepare children to be eager and ready to learn when it is time for them to enter schooling. One of the main foci of QIS is on staff development—with informal training through workshops, formal training with a community college and four-year university, on-site coaching, and a scholarship and wage supplement program to entice practitioners to stay in the occupation.

QIS as developed and implemented at Palm Beach County is essentially a case where a lead agency, i.e., the Children's Services Council, collaborates with a host of external partners—including School District of Palm Beach County, Early Learning Coalition of Palm Beach County, Palm Beach Community College, Family Central, Inc. etc.—to develop and implement a staff development program for practitioners of early care and education. QIS had been implemented for five years when we conducted the evaluation.

Lack of Evaluation of QIS to Improve Staff Development

Almost all states have committed to developing and implementing Quality Improvement Systems similar to the one described above. There have been few evaluations to gain knowledge on how to improve these system-wide staff development programs with multiple foci and external service providers (Thornburg, Mayfield, Hawks, & Fuger, 2009; Zellman, Perlman, Le, & Setodji, 2008). Based on multiple years of evaluation, we will discuss what we have learned for improving such a large scale staff development program. We have analyzed survey data from practitioners, quality assessment data for QIS sites, children's school readiness assessment for both QIS and non-QIS children, and data on implementation and process from Palm Beach Community College and Children's Services Council of Palm Beach County.

What Have We Learned for Improving Staff Development Based on Our Evaluation?

1. Intensity and duration are important features of any staff development program. How to balance them depends on the content of staff development. We found that for career advisors who help practitioners navigate the educational and career ladders, intensity is more important than duration. However, for early learning coaches who work with practitioners in classrooms to improve practice, duration is more important than intensity. Balancing intensity and duration has implications for resource allocations.

We collected data from 144 practitioners who were involved in and received training from QIS. For early learning coaches, we conducted four multiple regression models to examine the absolute effects and relative effects of the early learning coaches program on improvement of job skills. We modeled the effects of (a) the number of hours per month working with early learning coaches (i.e., intensity), (b) the number of months working with early learning coaches (i.e., duration), and (c) the total number of hours working with early learning coaches (i.e., total amount of hours by multiplying hours/per month and number of months). All models included statistical control over background variables. We found that the effect of early learning coaches mainly comes from the number of months working with early learning coaches, a measure of program duration. It is estimated that one more month of working with early learning coaches led to 34% of a standard-deviation increase in perceived improvement of job skills. In other words, the longer QIS practitioners work with early learning coaches, the more improvement of job skills they report.

As to the effect of career advisors, we modeled in the same manner as for early learning coaches. However, we found exactly the opposite effect—the intensity, rather than duration, of working with a career advisor is more important. The number of times per year working with career advisors, a measure of program intensity, had statistically significant effects on the early childcare career of QIS practitioners, whereas the number of years working with career advisors—the measure of program duration—had no statistically significant effect. One more time within a year working with career advisors increased career impact by 22% of a standard deviation among QIS practitioners.

The above findings regarding early learning coaches and career advisors has implications for conducting QIS. For early learning coaches, duration, rather than intensity, matters for coaches to help practitioners improve their job skills. In other words, coaches need sufficient time to impact job skills of practitioners. Our finding is consistent with the increasing literature concluding that the staff development program has to be sustained to be effective (e.g., Darling-Hammond, 1995). Therefore, the most effective way to improve job skills of practitioners is for them to develop a long-term partnership with coaches. Policymakers and administrators need to make efforts to sustain early learning coaches program for a sufficient period of time. On the other hand, we found that intensity, rather than duration, matters for career advisors to make impact on early childhood education practitioners' career. Stated differently, advisors need to interact frequently with practitioners to advise on their career issues. Therefore, the most effective way to impact the career path of practitioners is for them to engage in intensive guidance and consultation with advisors, particularly during the initial years of a career when practitioners need guidance the most. Policymakers in this case need to provide resources and opportunities for an intensive interaction between advisors and practitioners at the very beginning.

2. Some areas are more intractable than others. Through the evaluation, we found that there is more improvement in areas such as "activities," "language-reasoning," "space and furnishing," "personal care routines" than in areas such as "program structure." It is important to have early wins in those more tractable areas. However, more resources should be allocated to those more intractable areas to make a difference.

We have assessment data on Early Childhood Environmental Rating Scale (ECERS) or Early Childhood Environmental Rating Scale Revised Version (ECERS-R) from 84 child care centers. We are able to compare the baseline assessment with the formal assessment about 12 months after a childcare site joining QIS. QIS used ECERS before April 2005 and ECERS-R after that. When we look at the ECERS data (before April 2005), among the six dimensions that ECERS measured—(a) space and furnishing, (b) personal care routine, (c) language-reasoning, (d) activities, (e) interaction, and (f) program structure—there was statistically improvement in only one area (i.e., activities) between the baseline assessment and the formal assessment.

When we analyzed the ECERS-R data (after April 2005), we found that there are statistically significant improvements on all six measures, between the baseline and the formal assessment. Specifically, (a) space and furnishing, (b) personal care routines, (c) interaction, and (d) program structure (in this order) show moderate improvement with effect size ranging from 0.43 to 0.37. Meanwhile, (a) activities and (b) language-reasoning show considerable improvement with effect size of 0.82 and 0.59, respectively. According to Rosenthal and Rosnow (1984), effect sizes more than 0.50 are considered as large, between 0.30 and 0.50 as moderate, and less than 0.30 as small in behavioral sciences.

Therefore, as to the issue of "intractability" of educational problems (Sarason, 1996, 2002; Shen & Ma, 2006), if we juxtapose findings regarding the improvement between the baseline assessment and formal assessment, we realize that some areas are more tractable, such as "activities," others are less tractable, such as "program structure." It is indeed much easier to change a few "activities" than improve the "program structure."

3. As to the effect of a staff development program, we have to be patient. Through rigorous evaluation, we found that it takes time to see the results and the rate of improvement has been accelerating. In other words, the rate of improvement keeps increasing year by year, over a five-year span. It takes time to synchronize the components of a staff development program with multiple external partners, and the staff development program has become more and more efficient over the years.

The juxtaposition of the ECERS and ECERS-R data also points to the finding that it takes time to see the result of the program. During the early stage of QIS before April 2005, there was statistically significant improvement in only one area between the baseline and formal assessment while the data from after April 2005 indicate that there are statistically significant improvements in all six areas. Therefore, it appears that it takes time to improve the quality of childcare sites as measured by ECERS and ECERS-R. As a matter of fact, we conducted a test to specifically investigate whether those sites entering QIS later would experience a great amount of improvement in the same amount of time, i.e., after joining QIS for one year. We found that in comparison with the QIS sites that entered QIS one year earlier, entering the QIS one year later would move a childcare site up about 0.86 units more on a measurement scale of 1 to 7, on the overall measure of quality of early childhood education. In other words, QIS is becoming more efficient in improving the quality of childcare sites. Those entering QIS later show a larger amount of improvement between the baseline and the formal assessment. Thus, when we conduct staff development program, we should be flexible about our change efforts based on the feedback, but we must be persistent in our efforts.

4. The staff development program has differential impacts on various groups of practitioners. Minority practitioners are as likely to participate in informal training, but they are much less likely to participate in formal training and even much less likely to report a change in degree and certification level. Additional support is needed for certain groups of practitioners in order to achieve equitable results.

We surveyed 144 and 184 practitioners on two different occasions. Our results indicated that in comparison to their White counterparts, Hispanic practitioners benefited the most from early learning coaches, and both Black and Hispanic practitioners benefited more from career advisors. However, Black and Hispanic practitioners were less likely to report an improvement in level of degree or certification in early childcare and education than their White counterparts. Our analysis indicated that White QIS practitioners were about 12 times as likely to pursue change in the level of certification or degree as both Black and Hispanic QIS practitioners. There appear to be more barriers for Black and Hispanic practitioners in terms of educational preparation and financial resources. Thus, from the policy perspective, more encouragement and support should be given to minority practitioners to engage in staff development and pursue advancement in certification and degree levels.

5. Leadership plays an important role in the effectiveness of a staff development program. The evaluation data clearly indicate that when practitioners have their directors' encouragement and support, they are much more likely to apply what they have learned in the staff development program.

Leadership development is important for further enhancing the impact of QIS. Our survey with practitioners indicated that 82% of the practitioners reported that their directors were supportive of their training. Our further regression analyses of the data revealed that the support and encouragement from site directors are found to be positively associated with the level at which practitioners implement what they have learned in the training programs, a finding that is consistent with the literature on the role of leadership to facilitate educational change (Marzano, Waters, & McNulty, 2005; Shen, 1999). Therefore, leadership development is a crucial mediating factor to enhance the impact of QIS. When planning and implementing staff development programs, those in leadership roles should always be brought on board so that they could support and encourage practitioners in their innovative efforts.

6. It is crucial to understand the difference between outcome and impact. Outcomes are directly related to the staff development activities while impact is the long-term effect associated with the outcomes. For the staff development program we evaluated, the outcomes are related to practitioners' qualifications and practices as well as the quality of the childcare sites (addressed by the staff development program directly), while impact is related to children's school readiness (addressed by the program indirectly). We found that effects of positive outcomes related to practitioners and sites are large and emerge earlier, while the positive impacts on children's school readiness are small and take time to emerge. Therefore, it is important to communicate with stakeholders regarding a logic model that goes from issues/opportunities, to staff development activities that address the issues/opportunities, to outcomes directly related to the staff development activities, and finally to the impacts that are indirectly related to the staff development activities.

According to the logic model, QIS's direct outcomes are related to improving the qualification and practice of the practitioners, and the quality of childcare sites. As a result of the improvement of practitioners and sites, we would expect to see an improvement in impact on children's school readiness. What we learned from the evaluation is that QIS effect is attenuated when going from (a) the outcomes related to the quality of the practitioners and sites to (b) the impact related to children's school readiness.

The evaluation clearly indicates that practitioners benefit from the informal and formal training very early on, improve their degree and certification level, and are more likely to remain with the current sites. The evaluation data also indicate that for the first two years, QIS improved the quality of the childcare sites in isolated areas, but later on the quality of the childcare sites has been improved dramatically in all areas and the rate of improvement has accelerated over the years.

However, the evaluation data on children's school readiness indicate that when we compared the children's school readiness for 2006–07, 2007–08, and 2008–09 respectively, there was no difference between the QIS and non-QIS sites, with or without control for site characteristics. Nonetheless, when we went beyond cross-sectional comparison year by year, and investigated the growth rate for QIS and non-QIS sites between 2006–07 and 2008–09, QIS sites showed significant more growth in certain areas of children's school readiness. As a matter of fact, as far as "initial sound fluency" (i.e., a measure of school readiness) is concerned, the rate of growth of QIS sites was 5.80 percentage points higher than that of non-QIS sites over a period of three years. Similarly, QIS sites grew significantly slower than non-QIS sites in terms of the probability of being labeled as a Low Performing Provider, a designation given to the lowest 15% of the childcare sites by Florida Department of Education's Voluntary Pre-kindergarten Program based on an overall score for each site. The probability of being identified as Low Performing Provider grew three times faster for non-QIS sites, compared with QIS sites, over the course of three years.

The above data clearly indicate the importance of (a) distinguishing the direct and relatively short-term outcome, versus the indirect and long-term impact, and (b) the phenomenon of attenuation of effect from the outcome to the impact, where effects of outcomes are large and emerge earlier, while the impacts on children's school readiness are small and take time to emerge.

7. It is important to conduct rigorous evaluation of staff development program. Evaluation is constructive in helping improving the staff development program. The above lessons, among others, are testaments to the importance of using evaluation data to continuously improve the staff development program.

For the QIS evaluation we conducted, we have seen several important benefits associated with conducting the evaluation. First, evaluation can help improve the staff development program. Based on the finding on the intensity of career advisors, the program staff reallocates the funds to strengthen the up-front intensity for the interaction with career advisors. Based on the finding of the differential impact on White and ethnic minority practitioners, additional efforts have been made by the staff to seek resources to address financial barriers for ethnic minority practitioners. Second, evaluation has helped the project manage the political environment of the staff development program. In this culture of instant gratification, we see so often that an organization will jump from one staff development program to another quite frequently. Our evaluation clearly shows that it takes time to see the improvement, and the improvement accelerates over the years, a finding that helps protect the staff development program and deepen its implementation. Finally, evaluation also is a tool to strengthen the accountability of the program. For a program such as QIS, ultimately questions have been asked on the impact on children's school readiness. The evaluation data that show the progression from (a) the outcomes related to practitioners and childcare sites to (b) the impact on children's school readiness (Ma, Shen, Kavanaugh, Lu, Brandi, Goodman, Till & Watson, 2011; Ma, Shen, Lu, Brandi, Goodman & Watson, 2013; Shen, Ma, Tackett, Lu, Brandi, Goodman, Till & Watson, 2011), help address the issues of management, improvement, and ultimately accountability.

References

Belfield, C. R. (2004). *Early education: How important are the cost savings to the school system?* New York: Teachers College.

Darling-Hammond, L. (1995). Teacher learning that supports student learning. *Educational Leadership, 55*, 6–11.

Espinosa, l. M. (2008). *Challenging common myths about young English language learners.* New York: Foundation for Child Development.

Friendly, M., Doherty, G., & Beach, J. (2006). *Quality by design: What do we know about quality in early learning and child care, and what do we think? A literature review.* Toronto, Canada: Childcare Resource and Research Unit, University of Toronto.

Isenberg, J., & Renck-Jalongo, M. (2003). Major trends and issues in early childhood education: Challenges, controversies, and insights. New York: Teachers College, Columbia University.

Ma, X., Shen, J., Kavanaugh, A., Lu, X., Brandi, K., Goodman, J., Till, L., & Watson, G. (2011). Effects of quality improvement system on child care centers. *Journal of Research in Childhood Education, 25* (4) 399–414.

Ma, X., Shen, J., Lu, X., Brandi, K., Goodman, J., & Watson, G. (2013). Can quality improvement system improve childcare site performance in school readiness? *Journal of Educational Research, 106* (2), 146–156.

Marzano, R.J., Waters, T., McNulty, B.A. (2005). *School leadership that works.* Alexandria, VA: Association for Supervision and Curriculum Development.

Nelson, A. (2006). Closing the gap: Early childhood education. *Info Brief, 45,* 1–8.

Pittard, M., Zaslow, M., Lavelle, B., & Porter, T. (2006). *Investing in quality: A survey of state child care and development fund initiatives.* Washington, DC & New York: National Association of State Child Care Administrators, the Bank Street College of Education, & Child Trends.

Rosenthal, R., & Rosnow, R. L. (1984). *Essentials of behavioral research: Methods and data-analysis.* New York: McGraw-Hill.

Sarason, S.B. (1996). *Revisiting "The Culture of the School and the Problem of Change."* New York: Teachers College Press.

Sarason, S.B. (2002). *Educational reform: A self-scrutinizing memoir.* New York: Teachers College Press.

Shen, J. (1999). Connecting educational theory, research, and practice: John I. Goodlad's research. *Journal of Thought, 34* (4), 25–96.

Shen, J., & Ma, X. (2006). Does systemic change work? Curricular and instructional practice in the context of systemic change. *School Leadership and Policy 5* (3), 231–256.

Shen, J., Ma, X., Tackett, W., Lu, X., Brandi, K., Goodman, J., Till, L., Watson, G. (2011). Effects of quality improvement system on early childhood education practitioners. *Research and Practice Advances in Early Education and Day Care, 15,* 129–154.

Shlay, A.B., Tran, H., Weinraub, M., & Harmon, M. (2005). Teasing apart the child care conundrum: A factorial survey analysis of perceptions of child care quality, fair market price and willingness to pay by low-income, African American parents. *Early Childhood Research Quarterly, 20* (4), 393–416.

Shonkoff, J.P., & Phillips, D.A. (eds.). (2000). *From neurons to neighborhoods: The science of early childhood development.* Washington, DC: National Academy Press.

Takanishi, R., & Kauerz, K. (2008). PK inclusion: Getting serious about a P-16 education system. *Phi Delta Kappa,* 89, 480–87.

Thornburg, K. R., Mayfield, W. A., Hawks, J. S., & Fuger, K. L. (2009). *The Missouri quality rating system school readiness study.* Columbia, MO: Center for Family Policy & Research.

Zellman, G. L., Perlman, M., Le, V., & Setodji, C. M. (2008). *Assessing the validity of the Qualistar early learning quality rating and improvement system as a tool for improving child-care quality.* Santa Monica, CA: RAND.

Index

D

E

K

L

M

N

O

P

Q

R

S

T

U

V

W

X

Y

Z

www.ingramcontent.com/pod-product-compliance
Ingram Content Group UK Ltd.
Pitfield, Milton Keynes, MK11 3LW, UK
UKHW021851100926
8556IPUK00020B/1165

9 781433 120855